SPANISH EVERY DAY

A Learning Adventure for Young Readers

William C. Harvey

Illustrations: Dre Design
Denise Gilgannon

BARRON'S

For Valerie and Joanna

All inquiries should be addressed to:
Barron's Educational Series, Inc.
250 Wireless Boulevard
Hauppauge, New York 11788
http://www.barronseduc.com

ISBN-13: 978-0-7641-1694-0
ISBN-10: 0-7641-1694-0

Library of Congress Catalog Card Number 2001086498

Printed in the United States of America

15 14 13 12 11 10 9

CONTENTS

ABOUT THE AUTHOR

William C. Harvey is the author of many books, and has been teaching both Spanish and English for more than 20 years. His books and classes are fun because he makes learning easy for everyone. He wrote *Spanish Every Day* because he wanted boys and girls to know how exciting learning Spanish can be!

A NOTE TO PARENTS

Remind your young readers of the special features found in *Spanish Every Day*. They are located at the back of the book:

English-Spanish Vocabulary Lists
Cutout Vocabulary Flashcards

If you purchased the book and cassette kit, make sure that they listen to the cassette as often as possible. It is easy to follow along, since all Spanish words are practiced on the tape in the same order that they are presented in the book.

1 CHAPTER
UNO

Aprendamos español

(Let's Learn Spanish)

YOUR NEW FRIEND

This is Mister **Amigo**. He speaks both SPANISH and English. You can find him on many pages in this book. He will give you secrets about SPANISH, so that you can learn it easily—and very fast! Why don't you color him and all the drawings in this book?

ABOUT THIS BOOK

Today is a very special day. You are going to learn a new language called SPANISH.

The language you speak is called English. But many people in the world don't speak English. They speak other languages—like French, Chinese, or SPANISH!

This book will teach you how to understand and speak SPANISH. If you learn a little SPANISH every day, soon you will know two languages instead of one!

ABOUT THE TAPE

This book is sold with or without a cassette. If you got it with the tape, listen to it as you read this book, and stop it when you finish reading. Don't worry, the tape will tell you the page number!

Here are the many countries where people speak SPANISH.
Each country has a number. Take a pencil and draw a line from
the number of the country you see on the map to the same
number on the list. You *may* ask for help!

SPAIN (1)
MEXICO (2)
CUBA (3)
PUERTO RICO (4)
ARGENTINA (5)
GUATEMALA (6)
PERU (7)

EL SALVADOR (8)
COLOMBIA (9)
BOLIVIA (10)
URUGUAY (11)
CHILE (12)
COSTA RICA (13)
DOMINICAN REPUBLIC (14)

ECUADOR (15)
NICARAGUA (16)
HONDURAS (17)
VENEZUELA (18)
PARAGUAY (19)
PANAMA (20)

This book also has a VOCABULARY LIST of SPANISH and ENGLISH words. Whenever you forget how to say something, you can look it up in the VOCABULARY LIST, which is found at the back of this book.

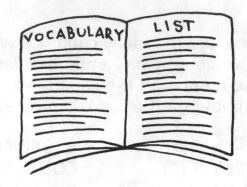

Start now by looking up the word "SPANISH." Write the word here:

_____

(To check your answer, look at the upside-down word below)

ANSWER: español

Good! Now, are you all set to learn more about the SPANISH language?

Let's begin with the most important part of all . . .

THE SUPER SOUNDS OF SPANISH

These are the five most important sounds of SPANISH. Once you learn them, you will be able to understand, speak, and read SPANISH words correctly.

The letters look just like English, but in SPANISH they have a very different sound. Go ahead, say each one aloud three times.

A (like "ah") The doctor tells the boy to say "ah."

E (like "eh") The man who cannot hear well says "eh."

I (like "ee") The girl who is scared says "ee."

O (like "oh") The lady who is surprised says "oh."

U (like "oo") At night the owl says "oo."

Here's what these SUPER SOUNDS look like inside SPANISH words.
Can you say each one correctly?

amigo

mucho

grande

Do you know what these words mean in English?
Look them up in the VOCABULARY LIST if you need to.

Let's learn some other sounds in SPANISH.
Practice each word three times, and notice what it means in English!

The letter **J** sounds like an "H":

jabón soap

jirafa giraffe

juego game

The letter **H** in Spanish has no sound at all:

hola hello

huevo egg

hombre man

The letter **Z** sounds just like an "S":

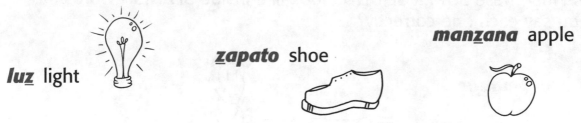

manzana apple

zapato shoe

luz light

And the letter **V** in SPANISH sounds more like a "B":

pavo turkey

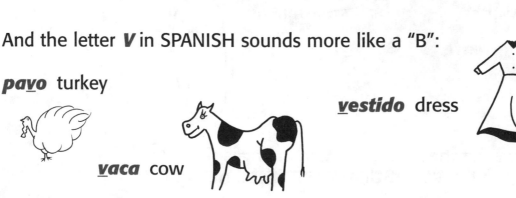

vestido dress

vaca cow

6

Remember that people will understand you even if your words aren't perfect, so just do the best you can!

Go ahead—write the correct SPANISH word next to each picture:

_____

_____

_____

_____

_____

Some SPANISH sounds are a little harder to say. These letters look funny, so be careful when you read each word aloud:

The SPANISH letter **LL** sounds a lot like a "Y":

*si**ll**a* chair

*amari**ll**o* yellow

*caba**ll**o* horse

7

The SPANISH letter **Ñ** sounds like "NY" in the word "CA<u>NY</u>ON":

Señorita (Srta.)
young lady (Ms.)

Señora (Sra.)
lady (Mrs.)

Señor (Sr.)
man (Mr.)

When together, the letters **QU** sound like a "K":

poquito a little bit

chiquito tiny

chaqueta jacket

Let's practice. You learned all of these words earlier. Fill in the missing letters, and then read everything aloud:

po__u__ __o   cha__ __ et__

a__ari__ __o   si __ __ a

__spa__ol   ca__al__o

__hiq__ __ to   s__ño__a

__est__do   j__eg__

8

RR is another letter in SPANISH that is very different from ENGLISH. To say it right, you must "roll your Rs," which sounds a lot like a car motor—RRRRRR!! Try to read these words the best you can:

ca_rr_o car

pe_rr_o dog

bu_rr_o donkey

Look at this funny picture. Name everything you see in SPANISH:

ANSWERS: *perro, vestido, carro, vaca, pavo*

Look how some SPANISH words have a little slanted line over a letter, like this ó. This tells us *to say that part of the word louder* than the other parts.

María	**Mary**
José	**Joe**
adiós	**good-bye**

A GUIDE TO SPEAKING SPANISH

1. **SPANISH words are pronounced exactly the way they are written.**

2. **Knowing the vowels (A, E, I, O, and U) is the secret to understanding and speaking SPANISH.**

3. **People will still understand you even if you don't say every SPANISH word correctly.**

4. **Say the accented (') part of a word a little louder. When the SPANISH word has no written accent, it is spoken louder at the end, unless it ends in A, E, I, O, U, N, or S.**

5. **REMEMBER: Your SPANISH will get better only if you speak it EVERY DAY . . !!**

SPANISH WORDS YOU ALREADY KNOW

These next words are fun to practice because they are exactly the same in both languages. But remember—they sound different when you say them in *español*:

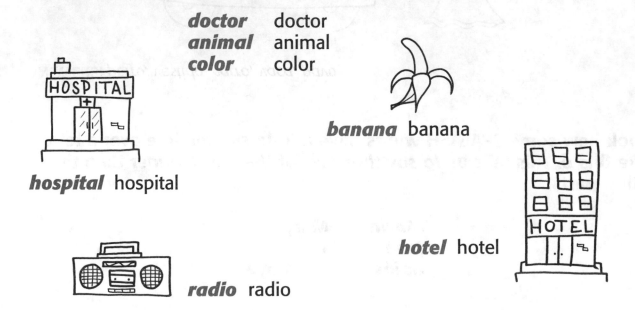

doctor doctor
animal animal
color color

banana banana

hospital hospital

hotel hotel

radio radio

Let's keep reading aloud. Say all of these SPANISH words correctly:

taco	*Los Angeles*
rodeo	*Florida*
salsa	*San Francisco*
chocolate	*Colorado*
tortilla	*Nevada*

If you're having trouble, be sure to review pages 5 through 9.

Now, underline all the SPANISH words you can find in the story below:

Juan is a doctor at a hospital in Los Angeles. He loves big tortilla tacos with lots of salsa. His favorite hotel in Florida sells chocolate bananas. He listens to the rodeo on the radio when he goes to Colorado.

ANSWERS:
Juan is a doctor at a hospital in Los Angeles. He loves big tortilla tacos with lots of salsa. His favorite hotel in Florida sells chocolate bananas. He listens to the rodeo on the radio when he goes to Colorado.

EASY SPANISH WORDS

Look at this list of SPANISH words. Most people learn them first because they are easy to remember:

nada	nothing
sí	yes
amigo	friend
mucho	a lot
gracias	thank you
bueno	good
grande	big

adiós good-bye

agua water

dinero money

casa house

fiesta party

chico small

You saw these words before. Can you remember what they mean?

señorita	<u>young lady</u>
hola	_____
zapato	_____
hombre	_____
carro	_____

ANSWERS: hello, shoe, man, car

12

This time, connect each word with its opposite:

chico	*sí*
hola	*señora*
poquito	*grande*
no	*adiós*
señor	*mucho*

WHAT'S YOUR NAME IN SPANISH?

Did you know that kids' names in SPANISH are different than in English? Read this list of people's names in SPANISH and practice every sound. If your name is not on the list, it's still okay; most people who speak SPANISH will call you by your real name anyway!

Los Nombres
(Names)

Los niños
(Boys)

Bobby	*Roberto*
Charlie	*Carlos*
Eddie	*Eduardo*
Frank	*Francisco*
George	*Jorge*
Jerry	*Geraldo*
Henry	*Enrique*
Jimmy	*Jaime*
John	*Juan*
Mark	*Marcos*
Nick	*Nicolás*

Tony	*Antonio*
Mike	*Miguel*
Peter	*Pedro*
Joey	*José*
Richard	*Ricardo*
Paul	*Pablo*
Steven	*Esteban*
Billy	*Guillermo*
Fred	*Federico*
Tom	*Tomás*
Andy	*Andrés*
Matthew	*Mateo*

Las niñas
(Girls)

Alice	*Alicia*
Betty	*Beatriz*
Anne	*Ana*
Carol	*Carolina*
Ellen	*Elena*
Jane	*Juana*
Cathy	*Catalina*
Susan	*Susana*
Lynn	*Lina*
Margaret	*Margarita*
Sarah	*Sara*
Hope	*Esperanza*
Lucy	*Luz*
Christy	*Cristina*
Mary	*María*
Grace	*Graciela*
Eve	*Eva*
Valerie	*Valeria*
Rose	*Rosa*
Julie	*Julia*

Watch out for these SPANISH names—they look just like English, but they are pronounced differently!

Daniel   **David**
Gloria   **Laura**
Samuel   **Víctor**
Linda   **Patricia**

Learn how to ask for people's names in SPANISH. Try this with someone right away!

What's your name?   ***¿Cómo te llamas?***
My name is . . .   ***Me llamo . . .***

MORE THINGS TO SAY IN *ESPAÑOL*

Speak a different language with your family and friends! Say these things today in SPANISH instead of English:

¡Hola!
Hi!

Con Permiso.
Excuse me.

Por Favor.
Please.

Muchas gracias.
Thanks a lot.

De nada.
You're welcome.

¿Cómo estás?

How are you?

Muy bien, gracias.¿Y tú?

Very well, thanks. And you?

¿Qué pasa?

What's going on?

Sin novedad.

Not much.

¡Adiós!

Good-bye!

¡Hasta luego!

See you later!

By the way, whenever you write a sentence in SPANISH, add an upside-down mark like this one: ¿ in front of a question, and ¡ in front of an exclamation.

¿Cómo estás?   **¡Bien!**

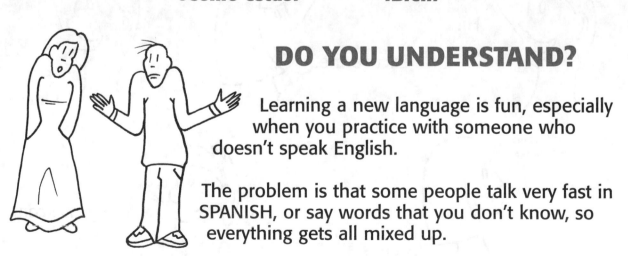

DO YOU UNDERSTAND?

Learning a new language is fun, especially when you practice with someone who doesn't speak English.

The problem is that some people talk very fast in SPANISH, or say words that you don't know, so everything gets all mixed up.

Here are some things you can say in SPANISH so that everybody will understand one another:

I'm sorry.   *Lo siento.*

Please speak more slowly.   *Habla más despacio, por favor.*

I'm learning SPANISH.   *Estoy aprendiendo español.*

I speak a little.   *Hablo un poco.*

Do you speak Spanish?

Do you understand?

Do you know?

I don't understand.

I don't know.

I don't remember.

To learn more things to say in SPANISH, look at the VOCABULARY LIST at the end of the book.

Don't forget these:

Good morning   *Buenos días.*
Good afternoon.   *Buenas tardes.*
Good night.   *Buenas noches.*

17

Let's practice some more:

Put SPANISH words in these balloons, and make the people talk to each other!

Now, connect the words that go together best.
And when you're done, read all of your answers aloud!

¡Hasta luego!	*Me llamo José.*
Muchas gracias.	*Muy bien.*
¿Cómo estás?	*Sin novedad.*
¿Qué pasa?	*¡Adiós!*
¿Hablas español?	*Sí, un poco.*
¿Cómo te llamas?	*De nada.*

ANSWERS: *¡Hasta luego!—¡Adiós!*
Muchas gracias.—De nada.
¿Cómo estás?—Muy bien.
¿Qué pasa?—Sin novedad.
¿Hablas español?—Sí, un poco.
¿Cómo te llamas?—Me llamo José.

Did you get them all correct? *¡Bueno!* If you had trouble, go back and read Chapter *UNO* again.

Whenever you're ready, go on to Chapter *DOS*. It's time for you to speak more SPANISH every day!

2 CHAPTER
DOS

En mi cuarto

(In My Room)

It's time to get up and speak SPANISH! When you wake up in the morning, what do you see?

pillow	*la almohada*
sheet	*la sábana*
bedspread	*la cubrecama*
pajamas	*la pijama*
clothes	*la ropa*

bed *la cama*

book *el libro*

blanket *la frazada*

stuffed animal
el animal de peluche

toy *el juguete*

Let's stop for a moment. Try making your bed in SPANISH! Unscramble these letters and practice each word:

l a b á s a a n _____

l a a c b a e c r u m _____

l a m a a c _____

l a z d a a a r f _____

l a h a l a m d a o _____

Okay, point to these things in the bedroom:

bookshelf   *el librero*
lamp   *la lámpara*
floor   *el piso*
chair   *la silla*
wall   *la pared*
ceiling   *el techo*

closet   *el ropero*

table   *la mesa*

window   *la ventana*

door   *la puerta*

dresser   *el tocador*

clock   *el reloj*

What Is *el* and What Is *la*?

Did you notice that in SPANISH the word *el* or *la* appears in front of words that name people and things?

Most of the time, words that end with *o* have *el* in front . . .

el libro   el piso   el radio   el amigo   el pavo

. . . while words that end in *a* have *la* in front:

la señora   la cama   la jirafa   la casa   la banana

And what do *el* and *la* mean? They mean "the"!

Put *el* or *la* in front of these other words, and then write the English:

el *juego*	the game
___ *manzana*	_____
___ *zapato*	_____
___ *huevo*	_____
___ *chaqueta*	_____
___ *vaca*	_____
___ *carro*	_____

ANSWERS: *la manzana* apple
el zapato shoe
el huevo egg
la chaqueta jacket
la vaca cow
el carro car

23

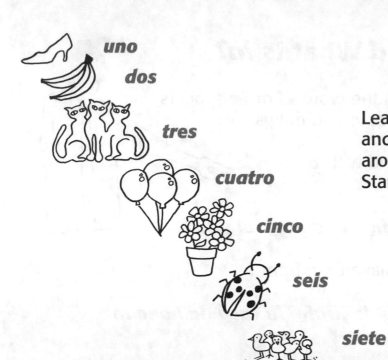

uno

dos

tres

cuatro

cinco

seis

siete

ocho

nueve

diez

Los números
(Numbers)

Learn the numbers in SPANISH, and you can count everything around you in two languages! Start with the numbers 1 to 10:

Fill in the missing number in SPANISH:

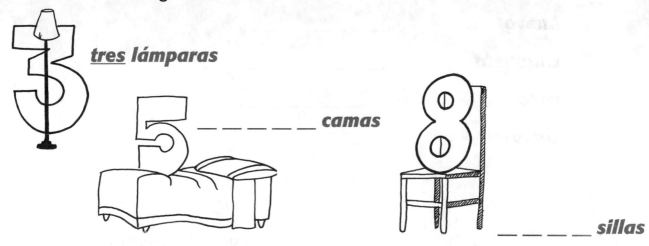

tres **lámparas**

_ _ _ _ _ _ _ **camas**

_ _ _ _ _ **sillas**

ANSWERS: *cinco camas, ocho sillas*

24

Now let's practice more *números* in SPANISH:

11	***once***
12	***doce***
13	***trece***
14	***catorce***
15	***quince***
16	***dieciséis***
17	***diecisiete***
18	***dieciocho***
19	***diecinueve***
20	***veinte***

Now that you know some *números*, try out this question right away!

How old are you?   I'm . . .
¿Cuántos años tienes?   ***Tengo . . .***

Write your age in SPANISH here: _____

These numbers are all mixed up. Take a minute to put them in order.
And be sure to read them aloud!

diez   uno   veinte   dieciocho   doce   tres

ocho   quince   diecisiete   cuatro   nueve

dieciséis   dos   cinco   catorce   siete

once   diecinueve   seis   trece

_____   _____   _____   _____   _____

_____   _____   _____   _____   _____

_____   _____   _____   _____   _____

_____   _____   _____   _____

26

Los juguetes
(Toys)

Do you have any toys in your bedroom? Be sure to count them in *español* !

game	*el juego*
puzzle	*el rompecabezas*
kite	*la cometa*
blocks	*los bloques*
robot	*el robot*
bat	*el bate*
ball	*la pelota*
glove	*el guante*
drum	*el tambor*
trumpet	*la trompeta*
skates	*los patines*

balloon *el globo*

rocket *el cohete*

doll *la muñeca*

soldier *el soldado*

train *el tren*

truck *el camión*

ship *el barco*

skateboard *la patineta*

guitar *la guitarra*

bicycle *la bicicleta*

You can also have fun with one of these:

computer *la computadora*

videos *los vídeos*

stereo *el estéreo*

Look for these toys in the WORD SEARCH puzzle below.

ESTEREO   **PATINETA**   **BICICLETA**
PELOTA   **GUANTE**   **TAMBOR**
JUEGO   **GLOBO**   **BATE**
SOLDADO   **TREN**   **BARCO**

Make sure you call out the word when you find it:

```
B   A   O   T   A   M   B   O   R   O   P
J   U   E   G   O   E   B   S   T   B   A
B   U   A   G   E   O   I   A   L   A   T
O   G   E   L   L   P   C   L   T   T   I
C   U   S   G   L   A   I   C   I   E   N
R   A   T   I   O   J   C   G   P   A   E
A   N   E   R   T   U   L   O   A   N   T
B   T   R   E   A   P   E   L   O   T   A
O   E   E   G   U   A   T   O   E   A   D
G   L   O   B   O   D   A   D   L   O   S
```

To talk about more than one thing in SPANISH, change the *el* to *los* . . .

the friend
el amigo

the friend**s**
los amigos

. . . and the *la* to *las* . . .

the lamp
la lámpara

the lamp**s**
las lámparas

Try some, and then check your answers:

the toy   *el juguete*

the toys   _____

the skateboard   *la patineta*

the skateboards   _____

ANSWERS: *los juguetes, las patinetas*

Now let's count a few toys together. How many do you see?

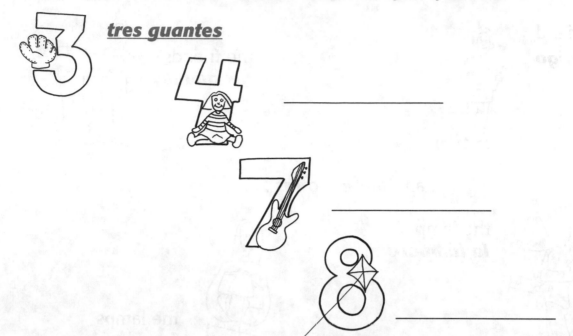

**tres guantes**

_____

_____

_____

Los animales de peluche
(Stuffed Animals)

Don't forget your favorite stuffed animals! Say their names slowly:

elephant   _**el elefante**_
lion   _**el león**_
rabbit   _**el conejo**_
tiger   _**el tigre**_

giraffe _**la jirafa**_

puppy _**el perrito**_

teddy bear _**el osito**_

dinosaur _**el dinosaurio**_

The Awesome Word *es*

The word **es** means "It's." Think of the thousands of sentences you can make in SPANISH with it!

It's the tiger.   *Es el tigre.*

It's the elephant.   *Es el* _____ .

It's the rabbit.   *Es* _____ .

It's the lion.   _____ .

It's the teddy bear.   _____ .

ANSWERS: *Es el elefante. Es el conejo. Es el león. Es el osito.*

Did You Say "My" *(mi)* or "Your" *(tu)*?

Practice saying "my" and "your" in SPANISH:

It's <u>my</u> elephant.   ***Es <u>mi</u> elefante.***
It's <u>your</u> giraffe.   ***Es <u>tu</u> jirafa.***

It's <u>my</u> tiger.   ***Es <u>mi</u> tigre.***
It's <u>your</u> lion.   ***Es <u>tu</u> león.***

Read these SPANISH words aloud and then write what they mean:

mi elefante   <u>my elephant</u>

catorce perritos   _____

los tigres   _____

tu jirafa   _____

dieciséis ositos   _____

ANSWERS: fourteen puppies, the tigers, your giraffe, sixteen teddy bears

¡Dime!
(Tell me!)

Tell your friends and family to do something in SPANISH, and soon, they will learn it too! Start in the bedroom. Call Mom or Dad, and tell her or him in SPANISH what to do! If they don't get it at first, show off by explaining it to them:

Touch . . .	*Toca . . .*	*. . . la cama*
		. . . la mesa
Point to . . .	*Señala . . .*	*. . . el libro*
		. . . la puerta
Look at . . .	*Mira . . .*	*. . . el juguete*
		. . . la silla

Follow these commands!

Toca el libro.
Mira la puerta.
Señala la cama.

Did you touch the book, look at the door, and point to the bed?
¡Muy bien! Now read the words below, and write what they
mean in English:

Toca los tres juguetes. _____

OK, do the same with these words.
But this time, you'll have to read them backwards first!

.satolep sies sal alañeS
Señala las seis pelotas.   Point to the six balls.

.senoel eveun sol ariM

_____   _____ .

.sarapmál sod sal acoT

_____   _____ .

Los colores
(The Colors)

Let's learn some colors in SPANISH. Point to things as you say each word:

blue   *azul*
black   *negro*
yellow   *amarillo*
brown   *café*
purple   *morado*

red *rojo*

white *blanco*

green *verde*

pink *rosado*

orange *anaranjado*

Use this question to practice the colors in SPANISH!

What color is it?
¿De qué color es?

El conejo es _____ .

¿De qué color es?

El _____ .

SPANISH words are put together differently. To say what color something is, put the color <u>after</u> the word instead of before.

Color these pictures as you read the words!

The <u>red</u> ball   *La pelota <u>roja</u>*
The <u>blue</u> truck   *El camión <u>azul</u>*
The <u>brown</u> dog   *El perro <u>café</u>*

Now there are two. Do you see the difference?

The <u>red</u> balls   *Las pelotas <u>rojas</u>*
The <u>blue</u> trucks   *Los camiones <u>azules</u>*
The <u>brown</u> dogs   *Los perros <u>cafés</u>*

Don't worry if you make mistakes when you practice.
You will get a little better every day!

Now, draw lines to connect these words all by yourself!

café	yellow
rosado	purple
blanco	red
azul	brown
anaranjado	black
amarillo	blue
negro	green
verde	white
rojo	orange
morado	pink

ANSWERS: *café* brown, *rosado* pink, *blanco* white, *azul* blue, *anaranjado* orange, *amarillo* yellow, *negro* black, *verde* green, *rojo* red, *morado* purple

Mi ropa
(My Clothes)

Before you leave the bedroom, put on your clothes in SPANISH!
Say these words every day when you need to get dressed:

I put on the . . .   *Me pongo . . .*
I take off the . . .   *Me quito . . .*

t-shirt	*la camiseta*
shirt	*la camisa*
shorts	*los pantalones cortos*
dress	*el vestido*
sweater	*el suéter*
shoes	*los zapatos*

pants *los pantalones*

socks *los calcetines*

skirt *la falda*

cap *la gorra*

jacket *la chaqueta*

belt *el cinturón*

And what do you wear when the weather is bad?

boots	*las botas*
overcoat	*el abrigo*
raincoat	*el impermeable*

What Is *un* and *una*?

This is how you say "a" or "an" in SPANISH.
Use *un* with words that end in *o*:

"UN" with "O"
and
"UNA" with "A"

A shoe   **_Un zapato_**
<u>An</u> overcoat   **_Un abrigo_**

And *una* with words that end in *a*:

<u>A</u> cap   **_Una gorra_**
<u>A</u> skirt   **_Una falda_**

Read these SPANISH words aloud:

It's a jacket.   **_Es una chaqueta._**
I put on a sweater.   **_Me pongo un suéter._**
It's a white shirt.   **_Es una camisa blanca._**

Put Them Together!

For fun, add the little word *y*, which means "and"
or the word *o*, which means "or":

"Y" is "AND"
and
"O" is "OR"

I put on a white shirt <u>and</u> a red sweater.
Me pongo una camisa blanca y un suéter rojo.

I take off the jacket <u>or</u> the cap.
Me quito la chaqueta o la gorra.

Look how much SPANISH you know!
Can you do this CROSSWORD PUZZLE?

ACROSS
1. socks
3. raincoat
7. pants

DOWN
1. t-shirt
2. sweater
4. boots
5. skirt
6. cap

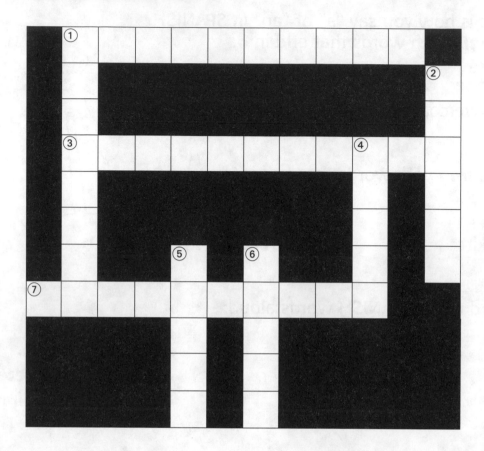

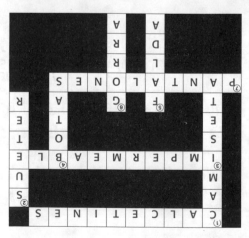

Let's practice what you've learned. Draw lines from the SPANISH sentences to the correct English sentences <u>and</u> read aloud:

Mira los zapatos rojos.	How old are you?
¿Cómo te llamas?	I put on my clothes.
Señala tu juguete.	What color is it?
¿Cuántos años tienes?	Look at the red shoes.
¿Entiendes?	What's happening?
Toca las dos sillas.	Point to your toy.
Es café y azul.	Do you understand?
¿Qué pasa?	It is brown and blue.
Me pongo mi ropa.	Touch the two chairs.
¿De qué color es?	What's your name?

Did you read everything aloud? *¡Muy bien!*

ANSWERS: *Mira los zapatos rojos.* Look at the red shoes.
¿Cómo te llamas? What's your name?
Señala tu juguete. Point to your toy.
¿Cuántos años tienes? How old are you?
¿Entiendes? Do you understand?
Toca las dos sillas. Touch the two chairs.
Es café y azul. It is brown and blue.
¿Qué pasa? What's happening?
Me pongo mi ropa. I put on my clothes.
¿De qué color es? What color is it?

You see—it's easy when you take the time to practice.

Now, let's leave the bedroom and learn more SPANISH every day . . .

3 CHAPTER
TRES

En mi casa

(In My Home)

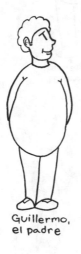

Guillermo,
el padre

María,
la madre

Francisco,
el hijo

Catalina,
la hija

Elena,
la abuela

Rubén,
el abuelo

La familia
(The Family)

Who do you see first in the morning?
Say **Buenos días** to these people every day:

mother   *madre*
wife   *esposa*

María,
la madre

father   *padre*
husband   *esposo*

Guillermo,
el padre

brother   *hermano*
son   *hijo*

Francisco,
el hijo

sister   *hermana*
daughter   *hija*

Catalina,
la hija

grandmother
abuela

Elena,
la abuela

grandfather
abuelo

Rubén,
el abuelo

42

It's easy to talk about the family:

Linda es mi hermana.   Linda is my sister.
Víctor es mi padre.   Victor is my father.

Now write the names of your family members:

_____ **es mi madre.**

_____ **es mi** _____ .

_____ .

Ask someone in your *familia* to practice SPANISH with you.
You read #1 while the other person reads #2:

#1: **Hola,** (the person's name).
#2: **Buenos días,** (your name).
#1: **¿Cómo estás?**
#2: **Bien, ¿y tú?**
#1: **Muy bien, gracias.**

One way to learn these words is to look at pictures of your family
and follow these commands:

	madre
Señala tu . . .	hermano
Mira tu . . .	padre
Toca tu . . .	abuelo
	hermana

To say "his" or "her" in SPANISH, use the little word **su**:

Linda es su hermana.   Linda is his sister.
Víctor es su padre.   Victor is her father.

¿Quién?
(Who?)

Look at the family on page 42, and then answer the questions below:

¿Quién es el padre? _____

¿Quién es la hija? _____

¿Quién es el hijo? _____

¡Muy bien! Now answer these questions about <u>your</u> family:

¿Cómo se llama tu padre? _____

¿Quién es tu madre? _____

¿Cómo está tu familia? _____

Underline every other letter to find out the secret message.
The first one is done for you:

a m o i s f t a b m u i r l m i n a e e l s o m d u a y l g o r s a t n a d r e .

¡Qué bonita!
(How pretty!)

What do the people in your family look like?
Say a few things about them as you move
through the house:

Es...
(He is... or She is...)

pretty   **bonito**
young   **joven**
good   **bueno**
ugly   **feo**
bad   **malo**
small   **chico**

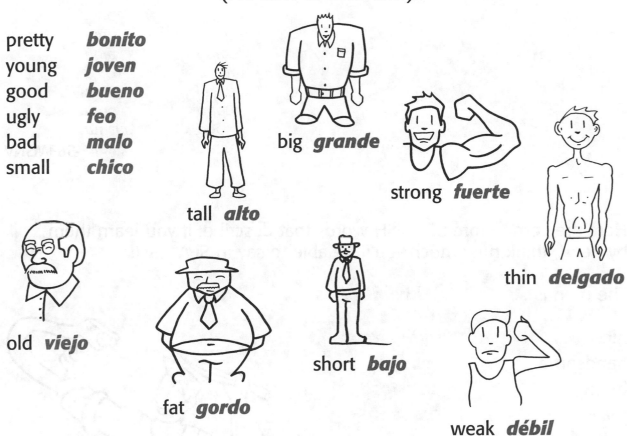

tall **alto**

big **grande**

strong **fuerte**

thin **delgado**

old **viejo**

fat **gordo**

short **bajo**

weak **débil**

Don't forget to change the final **o** to **a** when you talk about girls and
women! What do these words mean in English?

Mi padre es bajo y gordo,
y mi madre es alt_a_, delgad_a_ y bonit_a_.

ANSWER: My father is short and fat, and my mother is tall, thin, and pretty.

45

Connect the opposites!

blanco	*grande*
mucho	*bueno*
madre	*negro*
viejo	*adiós*
chico	*joven*
hola	*padre*
malo	*poco*

Here are some more SPANISH words that describe. If you learn them by heart, think how much you'll be able to say in SPANISH!

The man is . . .	*El hombre es . . .*
nice	*simpático*
handsome	*guapo*
funny	*chistoso*
brave	*valiente*
smart	*inteligente*

46

Put different names next to the words below. Think of famous people, friends, or even someone who lives in your house!

¡ _____ es muy bonita!

¡ _____ es muy valiente!

¡ _____ es muy chistosa!

¡ _____ es muy guapo!

¡ _____ es muy inteligente!

¡ _____ es muy fuerte!

Add the word *¡Qué...!* if you want to show surprise.
Write the English as you speak out loud:

¡Qué bonito!

How <u>pretty</u>!

¡Qué feo!

How _____ !

¡Qué chistoso!

How _____ !

¡Qué valiente!

How _____ !

ANSWERS: How ugly! How funny! How brave!

47

Él y ella
(He and She)

Let's learn how to say "he" and "she" in SPANISH.
Read all these words aloud:

John is my brother.   *Juan es mi hermano.*
He is small.   *<u>Él</u> es chico.*
He is very young.   *<u>Él</u> es muy joven.*

Mary is my sister.   *María es my hermana.*
She is funny.   *<u>Ella</u> es chistosa.*
She is very smart.   *<u>Ella</u> es muy inteligente.*

Put *Él* or *Ella* in place of the names below. The first one shows you how:

¿Dónde está <u>Sr. Smith</u>?   <u>*él*</u>

Mira a <u>Laura</u>.   _____

<u>Alicia</u> es una niña bonita.   _____

<u>David</u> es un hombre fuerte.   _____

¿Cómo está <u>Gloria</u>?   _____

ANSWERS: *ella, Ella, Él, ella*

48

Más de uno
(More than one)

If you want to describe more than one person or thing in SPANISH,
use the word *son* instead of *es:*

It's big.

Es grande.

They are big.

Son grandes.

Be sure to add *s* to the word that describes:

The man is tall.

El hombre es alto.

The men are tall.

Los hombres son altos.

Can you understand what these words mean?

Mis amigos son fuertes. _____ .

Tus abuelos son viejos. _____ .

Las niñas son inteligentes. _____ .

ANSWERS: My friends are strong.
Your grandparents are old.
The girls are smart.

49

This time, talk about many instead of only one:

Mi hermana es bonita.   <u>*Mis hermanas son bonitas.*</u>

Mi hermano es bueno.   _____.

Mi amiga es simpática.   _____.

So, when you describe, don't forget to add **s** when you talk of many things or people.

The <u>tall</u> man.   *El hombre <u>alto</u>.*
The <u>tall</u> men.   *Los hombres <u>altos</u>.*

Tú y yo
(You and I)

Let's learn how to say "you" and "I" in SPANISH.

Tú (You)   *Yo* (I)

50

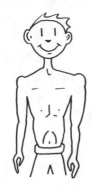

Use the word **Quién** (Who) to practice.
We learned all of these words earlier:

¿Quién es delgado?   <u>Yo</u>
(Who is thin?)

¿Quién es gordo?   <u>Tú</u>
(Who is fat?)

¿Quién es muy, muy inteligente?
(Who is very, very smart?)

_____

Connect the SPANISH word with its meaning:

Ella	He
Yo	You
Él	I
Tú	She

Bienvenidos a mi casa
(Welcome to My Home)

After you speak SPANISH to your family, go around the house and name everything you see:

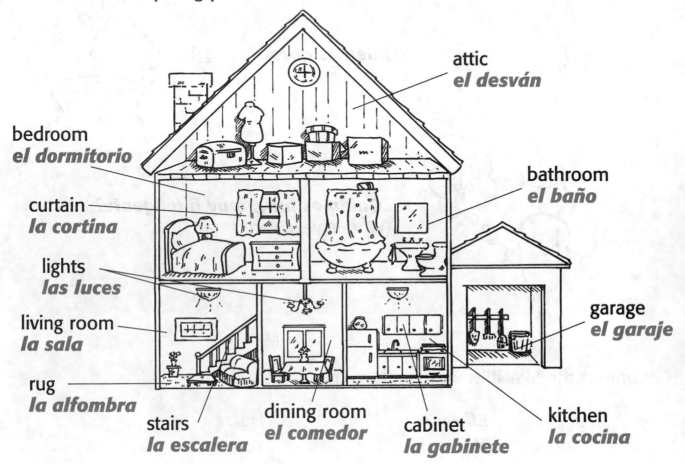

attic
el desván

bedroom
el dormitorio

curtain
la cortina

lights
las luces

living room
la sala

rug
la alfombra

stairs
la escalera

dining room
el comedor

cabinet
la gabinete

bathroom
el baño

garage
el garaje

kitchen
la cocina

Follow this new command!

Let's go to the . . .   *Vamos a . . .*

Let's go to the living room.   *Vamos a la sala.*
Let's go to the kitchen.   *Vamos a _____ .*
Let's go to the stairs.   *_____ .*

ANSWERS: *Vamos a la cocina.*
Vamos a la escalera.

52

Cross out the one word that doesn't belong with the others:

la ventana, la jirafa, las cortinas

el carro, el garaje, el hermano

el juguete, la cocina, el comedor

la lámpara, las luces, la falda

el libro, el piso, el techo

ANSWERS: *la jirafa, el hermano, el juguete, la falda, el libro*

¿Dónde está?
(Where is it?)

Use the word *está* to tell where something or someone is.

The book is on the table.
El libro <u>está</u> en la mesa.

My father is in his room.
Mi padre <u>está</u> en su cuarto.

Fill in the word *está* and write what the words mean in English:

Tony <u>está</u> en el comedor.   <u>Tony is in the dining room.</u>

Mi hermana _____ en el garaje.   _____ .

El baño _____ en la casa.   _____ .

La muñeca _____ en el piso.   _____ .

Tu camisa _____ en el dormitorio.   _____ .

ANSWERS: *My sister is in the garage. The bathroom is in the house. The doll is on the floor. Your shirt is in the bedroom.*

Use **están** when you are talking about more than one person or thing:

Where <u>are they</u>?
¿Dónde están?

<u>They are</u> in the bathroom.
Están en el baño.

Más cosas en la casa
(More Things in the House)

Move from room to room, learning the names for everything in SPANISH.
Write these words on little sticky notes. Then, stick them on the furniture
so you won't forget.

couch   ***el sofá***
refrigerator   ***el refrigerador***
dryer   ***la secadora***
trash can   ***el bote de basura***

desk ***el escritorio***

armchair ***el sillón***

stove ***la estufa***

washer ***la lavadora***

television ***el televisor***

Connect the English words with their meaning in SPANISH:

The washer is white. *El sillón es bonito.*
Where is the stove? *¿Dónde están las sillas?*
Your couch is in the house. *¿Dónde está la estufa?*
My desk is brown. *La lavadora es blanca.*
The armchair is pretty. *Mi escritorio es café.*
Where are the chairs? *Tu sofá está en la casa.*

ANSWERS:
The washer is white. *La lavadora es blanca.*
Where is the stove? *¿Dónde está la estufa?*
Your couch is in the house. *Tu sofá está en la casa.*
My desk is brown. *Mi escritorio es café.*
The armchair is pretty. *El sillón es bonito.*
Where are the chairs? *¿Dónde están las sillas?*

Now unscramble these letters and write what the words mean in English:

ESPAÑOL	ENGLISH
la raavload	_____
el veroteils	_____
la fuetas	_____

ANSWERS:
la lavadora washer
el televisor television
la estufa stove

55

Ellos y ellas
(They [Boys] and They [Girls])

When you say "they" referring to boys, men, and all the male animals, birds (and even fish!) you say *ellos*. And when you say "they" referring to girls, women, and all the female animals (and also fish!) you say *ellas*.

They are bulls.   *Ell**os** son tor**os**.*
They are boys.   *Ell**os** son niñ**os**.*

They are cows.   *Ell**as** son vac**as**.*
They are women.   *Ell**as** son señor**as**.*

Did you see the *as* and *os* endings?
Did you see how they match?

Aquí y allí
(Here and There)

"EN" means "IN"
"EN" means "ON"
"EN" means "AT"

Sometimes things in the house get moved around. These next SPANISH words will help you find what you're looking for.

Start with the word *en*, which can mean "in," "at," or "on":

Mi madre está en la cocina, en la mesa, en la silla.
My mom is <u>in</u> the kitchen, <u>at</u> the table, <u>on</u> the chair.

And look at these! (Keep reading aloud!)

up	*arriba*	behind *detrás*
inside	*adentro*	
in front	*enfrente*	
outside	*afuera*	

near *cerca*

under *bajo*

down *abajo*

above *encima*

far *lejos*

Finish these sentences with any of the words above:

It's _____ .   *Está* _____ .

They're _____ .   *Están* _____ .

Look at this picture. Write these words inside the balloons below.

detrás   **adentro**   **enfrente**   **afuera**

Where are they—***arriba*** or ***abajo***?

el piso   _____

las luces   _____

la alfombra   _____

el techo   _____

¿Cómo es?
(What does it look like?)

Use these words to describe the things in your *casa:*

full   *lleno*
expensive *caro*
cheap   *barato*
empty   *vacío*

clean *limpio*

new *nuevo*

hot *caliente*

old *vieja*

dirty *sucio*

cold *frío*

Read every word aloud!

El sillón es nuevo.	The armchair is new.
Las cortinas están limpias.	The curtains are clean.
La estufa está caliente.	The stove is hot.

¡Muy bien! Now finish these with the missing word:

It's dirty.   *Está* _____ .

It's full.   *Está* _____ .

It's cold.   *Está* _____ .

ANSWERS: *sucio, lleno, frío*

59

¿O o A?
(O or A?)

When you talk about a thing that ends in **o**, the word that describes it usually does too. Look:

El zapato es negro y bonito.
The shoe is black and pretty.

See? The name of the thing is **zapato**, so what we say about it should end in **o** (**negro, bonito**).

Also, if the name of the thing ends in **a**, then what we say about it often ends in **a**. Look:

La silla es negra y bonita.
The chair is black and pretty.

Let's see if you got it. Add **o** or **a** to the words that describe.

1. **La silla es barat__ y limpi__ .**

2. **El techo es blanc__ y bonit__ .**

3. **La alfombra es roj__ y morad__ .**

4. **La lámpara es fe__ y chic__ .**

5. **El librero es baj__ y viej__ .**

Now connect the opposites:

enfrente	**caro**
arriba	**lejos**
frío	**ella**
afuera	**allí**
él	**adentro**
cerca	**caliente**
barato	**detrás**
aquí	**abajo**

No! No! No!
(Not! Not! Not!)

Use **No** to say "NOT" in SPANISH. Watch:

It's clean.	**Está limpio.**
It's <u>not</u> clean.	**<u>No</u> está limpio.**
They're old.	**Son viejos.**
They're <u>not</u> old.	**<u>No</u> son viejos.**

You try one. Fill in the missing words:

My book is here.   **<u>Mi libro está aquí.</u>**

My book is not here. _____

Keep speaking SPANISH around the house. Can you guess what these words mean?

Mi familia está en la casa. La casa es blanca, azul, y grande. El garaje está enfrente de la casa. La familia no está en el garaje. Mi padre y mi madre están en la cocina. Ellos están cerca de la estufa y el refrigerador. Mis dos hermanos están en la sala. Son muy chistosos. Están enfrente del televisor. ¿Dónde está tu familia y cómo es tu casa?

ANSWERS: My family is in the house. The house is white, blue, and big. The garage is in front of the house. The family is not in the garage. My mother and father are in the kitchen. They are near the stove and the refrigerator. My two brothers are in the living room. They are very funny. They are in front of the television. Where is your family and what does your house look like?

These three questions are great for talking about your *casa.*
Go ahead—answer everything in *ESPAÑOL:*

Where do you live?   I live in _____ .

¿Dónde vives?   *Vivo en _____ .*

What's your address?   My address is _____ .

¿Cuál es tu dirección?   *Mi dirección es _____ .*

_____

_____

What's your phone number?   My number is _____ .

¿Cuál es tu número de teléfono?   *Mi número es _____ .*

But we're not finished yet!
Let's go to another part of the house
to learn more SPANISH every day . . .

4 CHAPTER CUATRO

A la cocina

(To the Kitchen)

grapes
las uvas

milk
la leche

watermelon
la sandía

eggs
los huevos

strawberries
las fresas

soda
los refrescos

ham
el jamón

fish
el pescado

cheese
el queso

meat
la carne

bread
el pan

butter
la mantequilla

juice
el jugo

oranges
las naranjas

¿Cómo estás?
(How are you?)

On your way to the kitchen, find out how everyone is feeling today:

I am . . .   *Estoy . . .*

fine *bien*

happy *feliz*

excited *emocionado*

Sometimes, we don't feel very well. Put in any word that fits:

Are you . . . ?   *¿Estás . . . ?*

sad *triste*

angry *enojada*

tired *cansada*

Use the words *estoy* and *estás* to talk about how you feel
and where you are.

Where are you?   *¿Dónde estás?*

I'm in the kitchen.   *Estoy en la cocina.*

Ask someone to read along with you.
Each person takes a different part:

#1 *¿Cómo estás?*
#2 *Estoy muy feliz, gracias.*
   Mis amigos están en mi casa.
   ¿Y tú?
#1 *Estoy muy triste.*
   Mis amigos no están bien.
#2 *¿Dónde están tus amigos?*
#1 *No están aquí. ¡Están en la cama!*

Do you know what you are saying?

Connect with lines the right picture with the right word:

cansada   *enojado*   *feliz*

Tengo mucha hambre
(I'm very hungry)

Does speaking SPANISH make you hungry? Go into the kitchen and find something to eat:

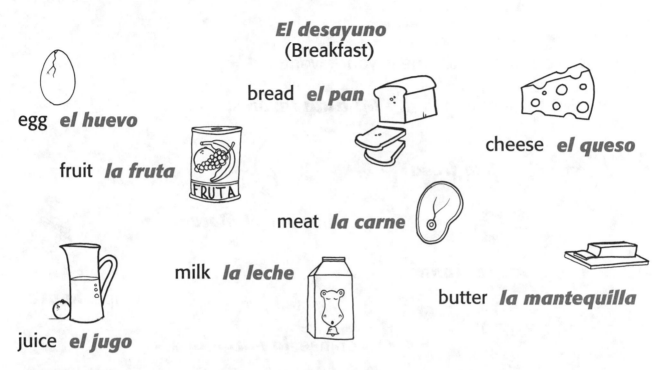

El desayuno
(Breakfast)

egg **el huevo**

bread **el pan**

cheese **el queso**

fruit **la fruta**

meat **la carne**

milk **la leche**

butter **la mantequilla**

juice **el jugo**

Use these new words EVERY DAY. Put anything you like on the left-hand lines below, and then see if you can write it in SPANISH on the right-hand ones:

Do you like _____ ? ☞ **¿Te gusta _____ ?**

Yes, I like _____ . ☞ **Sí, me gusta _____ .**

Do you want _____ ? ☞ **¿Quieres _____ ?**

Yes, I want _____ . ☞ **Sí, quiero _____ .**

Let's practice what we learned at breakfast. Fill in all the missing letters:

p _ n   _ ues _   _ ar _ e

h _ _ vo   _ r _ t _   _ ug _

ANSWERS: pan, queso, carne, huevo, fruta, jugo

Do you like fruit? Which one is your favorite?

My favorite fruit is …   *Mi fruta favorita es …*

 strawberry *la fresa*

 banana *el plátano*

 apple *la manzana*

 grape *la uva*

 orange *la naranja*

 watermelon *la sandía*

Be sure to add <u>color</u> to all these pictures!

Which one is bigger? Underline your answer:

la naranja o la uva

la manzana o la sandía

el plátano o la fresa

ANSWERS: la naranja, la sandía, el plátano

Esto y eso
(This and That)

Test yourself! Touch something and say:

What is <u>this</u>?   *¿Qué es <u>esto</u>?*

Then, point to something else and ask:

What is <u>that</u>?   *¿Qué es <u>eso</u>?*

Los vegetales
(Vegetables)

Open the refrigerator and look for any vegetables.
Take out each one as you practice aloud:

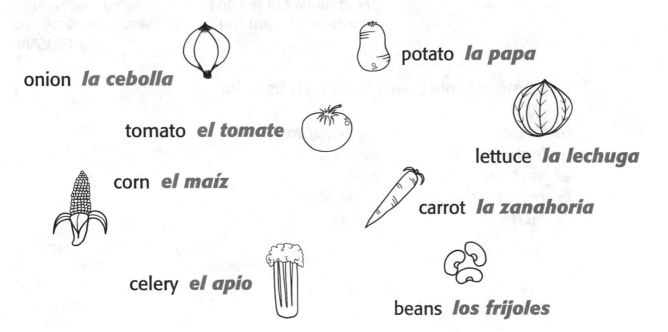

potato *la papa*

onion *la cebolla*

tomato *el tomate*

lettuce *la lechuga*

corn *el maíz*

carrot *la zanahoria*

celery *el apio*

beans *los frijoles*

You have a lot of words to remember. Connect the sentences that mean the same:

Me gusta la sandía.   The celery is thin.
Mira el pan blanco.   The juice is cold.
Las uvas son buenas.   I want my breakfast.
La papa es grande.   I like the watermelon.
Las naranjas están aquí.   The butter is there.
Los huevos son chicos.   Look at the white bread.
El jugo está frío.   The oranges are here.
La mantequilla está allí.   The grapes are good.
El apio es delgado.   The eggs are small.
Yo quiero mi desayuno.   The potato is big.

ANSWERS:
Me gusta la sandía.   I like the watermelon.
Mira el pan blanco.   Look at the white bread.
Las uvas son buenas.   The grapes are good.
La papa es grande.   The potato is big.
Las naranjas están aquí.   The oranges are here.
Los huevos son chicos.   The eggs are small.
El jugo está frío.   The juice is cold.
La mantequilla está allí.   The butter is there.
El apio es delgado.   The celery is thin.
Yo quiero mi desayuno.   I want my breakfast.

This time, connect each food with its color:

la fresa   *anaranjada*
la lechuga   *blanca*
el plátano   *roja*
la zanahoria   *amarillo*
la leche   *verde*

ANSWERS:
la fresa   *roja*
la lechuga   *verde*
el plátano   *amarillo*
la zanahoria   *anaranjada*
la leche   *blanca*

You will not go far if you don't know how to ask "How many?"
and "How much?"

How many?   *¿Cuántos?*

¿Cuántos plátanos?   *¿Dos o tres?*
¡Tres!

How much?   *¿Cuánto?*

¿Cuánta leche?   *¿Mucha o poca?*
¡Mucha!

Más comida
(More Food)

Call out these new commands in the kitchen.

Eat . . .
Come . . .

Take . . .
Toma . . .

Bring . . .
Trae . . .

El almuerzo
(Lunch)

hamburger *la hamburguesa*
salad *la ensalada*
soup *la sopa*

hot dog *el perro caliente*

french fries *las papas fritas*

sandwich *el sandwich*

71

La cena
(Dinner)

chicken **el pollo**
ham **el jamón**

turkey **el pavo**

fish **el pescado**

steak **el bistec**

Cross out the one word that doesn't belong with the other two:

leche, jugo, jamón

piso, pavo, pollo

lechuga, tomate, juguete

pescado, desayuno, almuerzo

manzana, camisa, naranja

toma, come, apio

ANSWERS: *jamón, piso, juguete, pescado, camisa, apio*

Choose the best word to finish the phrase:

ensalada   mantequilla   naranja

pan y _____

jugo de _____

sopa y _____

ANSWERS:
mantequilla
naranja
ensalada

Practice saying these with a friend today:

¿Tienes hambre?	*Sí, tengo mucha hambre.*
Are you hungry?	Yes, I'm very hungry.

¿Tienes sed?	*Sí, tengo mucha sed.*
Are you thirsty?	Yes, I'm very thirsty.

Las bebidas
(Drinks)

Ask your family in SPANISH! Use these questions:

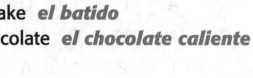

Do you like . . .	*¿Te gusta . . . ?*
Do you want . . .	*¿Quieres . . . ?*

lemonade *la limonada*
milk shake *el batido*
hot chocolate *el chocolate caliente*

tea *el té*

soda *el refresco*

Which do you like better? Circle your answer:

el agua o el batido

la leche o el refresco

el chocolate caliente o el té

Write three words under each category:

Los vegetales	*Las frutas*	*Las bebidas*
_____	_____	_____
_____	_____	_____
_____	_____	_____

Find these words in the WORD SEARCH puzzle below:

CARNE   PAN   LECHE   HUEVO   MANZANA   UVA

FRESA   TOMATE   PAVO   SOPA   APIO   REFRESCO

```
O  E  C  S  O  P  A  H  U  S
A  H  O  T  O  V  A  P  I  O
R  C  O  A  E  T  A  M  O  T
E  E  P  A  C  T  T  P  F  A
F  L  E  N  A  P  I  E  R  N
R  P  R  V  R  Z  H  A  E  A
E  F  O  T  N  C  A  P  S  Z
S  A  H  U  E  V  O  F  A  N
C  S  V  L  P  A  R  U  V  A
O  U  A  A  R  E  T  T  O  M
```

Here's another dialogue to practice:

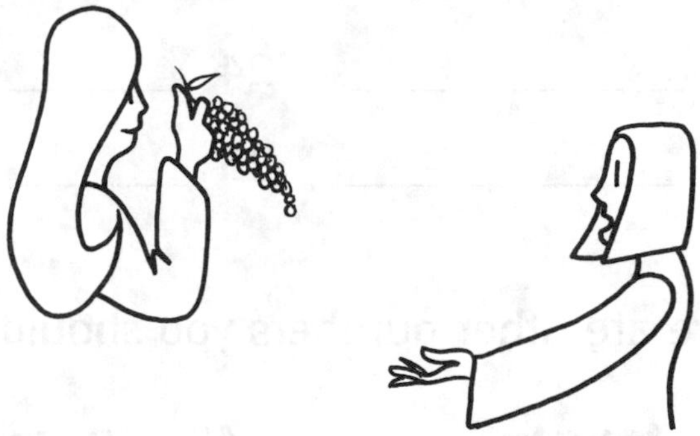

#1 ***¿Tienes hambre?***

#2 ***Sí, tengo mucha hambre.***
Vamos a la cocina.

#1 ***Muy bien.***
¿Te gusta la fruta?

#2 ***Sí, quiero las uvas, por favor.***

#1 ***¿Cuántas quieres?***

#2 ***¡Muchas!***

ANSWERS:
#1 Are you hungry?
#2 Yes, I'm very hungry. Let's go to the kitchen.
#1 Great. Do you like fruit?
#2 Yes, I want grapes, please.
#1 How many do you want?
#2 A lot!

Más números
(More Numbers)

You need to learn more numbers, so let's practice these words right now. First, count from one to twenty in SPANISH as fast as you can:

1, 2, 3, 4, 5, 6, 7, 8, 9, 10, 11, 12, 13, 14, 15, 16, 17, 18, 19, 20

¡Fantástico! To say 21, just put 20 and 1 together:

veinte y uno

Can you finish this list all by yourself?

22 _____   24 _____

23 _____   25 _____

Here are other numbers you should know:

30	*treinta*	40	*cuarenta*
50	*cincuenta*	60	*sesenta*
70	*setenta*	80	*ochenta*
90	*noventa*	100	*cien*

And what about all the numbers in between?

31 *treinta y uno*   55 *cincuenta y cinco*

72 _____   99 _____

ANSWERS: *setenta y dos*
noventa y nueve

Practice your numbers in SPANISH every day:

Find out the ages of everyone in your *familia*.

Count all the toys, books, or shoes in the *casa*.

Read every page number in this book in *español*.

¿Qué hora es?
(What time is it?)

After you eat, check the kitchen clock. It's easy to tell time in SPANISH. Just say the hour . . .

It's three o'clock.
***Son las* tres.**

It's eight o'clock.
***Son las* ocho.**

. . . and then add the minutes:

It's 3:10.
***Son las* tres y diez.**

It's 7:45.
***Son las* siete y cuarenta y cinco.**

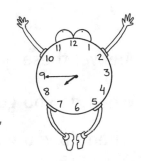

O.K. Connect each clock with the correct time:

Son las cuatro y quince.

Es la una.

Son las doce.

Son las siete y cuarenta y cinco.

Es la una y treinta.

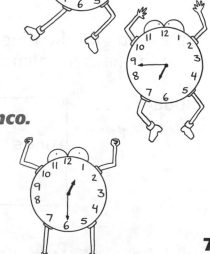

This is how you say "at" a certain time:

<u>At</u> 2:00
***A las* dos**

<u>At</u> 9:20
***A las* nueve y veinte**

<u>At</u> 5:05
***A las* cinco y cinco**

Answer these questions *en español* :

When do you go to bed?   ***A las*** _____ .

When do you go to school? ***A las*** _____ .

When do you wake up?   ***A las*** _____ .

¿Qué día es hoy?
(What day is today?)

After you give the time in SPANISH, tell everyone what day it is.
Use the kitchen calendar:

Today is . . .
Hoy es . . .

1	2	3	4	5	6	7
Lunes	Martes	Miércoles	Jueves	Viernes	Sábado	Domingo

These words are spelled backwards. Write them correctly, and then put them in the right order:

s e v e u j   *s e n u l*   *o g n i m o d*   *s e t r a m*

_____   _____   _____   _____

s e n r e í v   *s e l o c r é i m*   *o d a b á s*

_____   _____   _____

1. _____

2. _____

3. _____

4. _____

5. _____

6. _____

7. _____

¿Cuál es la fecha?
(What's the date?)

Learn these months and you will be able to say today's date in a different language!

January **enero**
February **febrero**
March **marzo**

July **julio**
August **agosto**
September **septiembre**

April **abril**
May **mayo**
June **junio**

October **octubre**
November **noviembre**
December **diciembre**

Be careful! In SPANISH, the number goes first:

Oct. 5th   el *cinco* de octubre
May 21st   el *veinte y uno* de mayo
Dec. 12th   el *doce* de diciembre

Learn these words, too:

week **la semana**   month **el mes**   year **el año**

Say in SPANISH:

June 15th

Sept. 30th

March 22nd

ANSWERS:
El quince de junio
El treinta de septiembre
El veinte y dos de marzo

80

Translate, and then answer the question:

¿Cuántos días en una semana? _____

¿Cuántos meses en un año? _____

Go look at the clock and calendar right now:

¿Qué hora es? _____

¿Qué día es hoy? _____

¿Cuál es la fecha? _____

¿Cuándo?
(When?)

Choose any of these words to talk about time:

today	*hoy*
tomorrow	*mañana*
yesterday	*ayer*
always	*siempre*
never	*nunca*
sometimes	*a veces*

Many SPANISH words can be learned in pairs:

before	*antes*	after	*después*
early	*temprano*	late	*tarde*

Ready to practice? Connect the opposites:

antes   **siempre**
nunca   **temprano**
ayer   **después**
tarde   **hoy**

ANSWERS: *antes* — *nunca* — *ayer* — *tarde*
después — *siempre* — *hoy* — *temprano*

These two <u>new</u> command words go well with the clock and the calendar:

Come . . .
Ven . . .

Go . . .
Anda . . .

. . . *a las ocho*
. . . *en tres semanas*
. . . *en enero*
. . . *temprano mañana*
. . . *en una hora*
. . . *antes de las cuatro*
. . . *en dos meses*
. . . *el miércoles*

Use this code to figure out the secret day of the year!

1	2	3	4	5	6	7	8	9	10	11	12	13	14	15	16	17	18	19	20	21	22	23	24	25
A	B	C	D	E	F	G	H	I	J	K	L	M	N	O	P	Q	R	S	T	U	V	W	X	Y

5-12   22-5-9-14-20-5   25   3-9-14-3-15   4-5   4-9-3-9-5-13-2-18-5

ANSWERS: *El veinte y cinco de diciembre* (CHRISTMAS!)

The kitchen is full of SPANISH, but there is still more to come.
If you want, read CHAPTER *CUATRO* one more time before moving ahead.
And don't forget—keep speaking SPANISH every day!

5 CHAPTER CINCO

Vamos afuera

(Let's Go Outside)

¿Qué tiempo hace?
(How's the weather?)

It's time to learn SPANISH outside the house. Start by saying something about the weather:

It's . . .   **Está . . .**

raining **lloviendo**
windy **ventoso**

cloudy **nublado**

snowing **nevando**

You can also use the word **Hace:**

It's . . .   **Hace . . .**

cold   **frío**
sunny   **sol**
hot   **calor**

Now, connect the words that mean the same:

It's snowing.   **Hace sol.**
It's sunny.   **Está lloviendo.**
It's raining.   **Está nevando.**

Draw this picture:

Es un día bonito. No está nublado. Hace mucho sol.

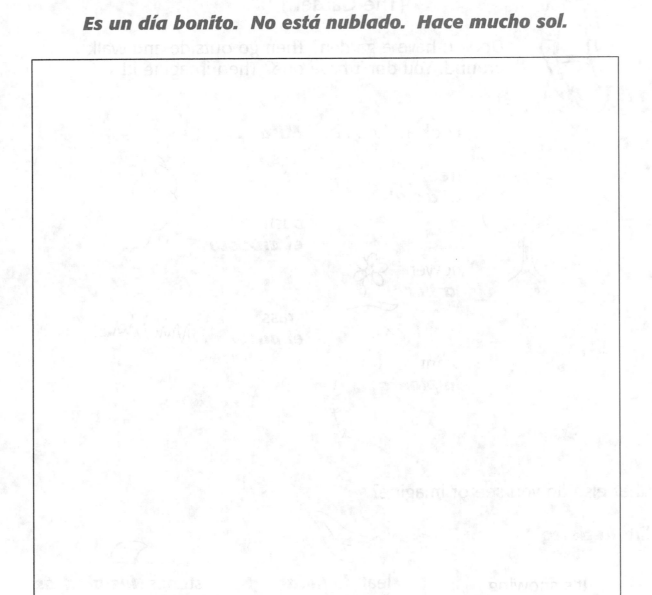

Look outside right now and say what you see:

Hace . . .   *Está . . .*

El jardín
(The Garden)

Do you have a garden? Then go outside and walk around. You don't have one? Then imagine it!

Look at the . . .   *Mira . . .*

tree
el árbol

bush
el arbusto

flower
la flor

grass
el pasto

plant
la planta

What else do you see or imagine?

dirt *la tierra*

leaf *la hoja*

stones *las piedras*

Color all these pictures today!

The little SPANISH word *Hay* means "There is" or "There are." It sounds like the word "I" in English:

There <u>is</u> a lot of dirt.   *Hay mucha tierra.*
There <u>are</u> a lot of stones.   *Hay muchas piedras.*

86

Put these words in order:

There is a lot of grass in the garden:

en   mucho   Hay   el jardín   pasto

_____

There are a lot of leaves on the bush:

el arbusto   hojas   Hay   en   muchas

_____

There are bugs and small animals in every garden. Point and speak:

Point to the. . .   *Señala . . .*

ant **la hormiga**

bee **la abeja**

spider **la araña**

fly **la mosca**   snail **el caracol**

Underline the word that doesn't fit:

calor, frío, palo
viento, mosca, abeja
arbusto, tiempo, árbol

Circle the correct answer:

Las hormigas son (*cocinas, calcetines, chicas*)
La flor es (*tierra, pelota, amarilla*)
Hace frío y está (*mesa, lloviendo, arbusto*)

Los animales domésticos
(House Pets)

Do you have pets around the house? Do your friends have any?
Look how different they are in SPANISH:

dog **el perro**

cat **el gato**

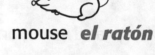

mouse **el ratón**

turtle **la tortuga**

bird **el pájaro**

Children who live on a farm play with these:

pig **el puerco**

horse **el caballo**

sheep **la oveja**

cow **la vaca**

duck **el pato**

Draw a line from each picture to the correct word:

la oveja　　　*el gato*　　　*el caballo*　　　*el pájaro*　　　*el perro*

Follow this maze through the garden.
Be sure you speak SPANISH along the way!

Trabajo en el jardín
(I work in the garden)

When you go to a garden, these commands will show how much you know:

Point to the . . .	*Señala . . .*
Look at the . . .	*Mira . . .*
Touch the . . .	*Toca . . .*
Bring the . . .	*Trae . . .*
Take the . . .	*Toma . . .*

shovel *la pala*

broom *la escoba*

ladder *la escalera*

rake *el rastrillo*

hose *la manguera*

Más herramientas
(More Tools)

pliers *las pinzas*
nail *el clavo*

hammer *el martillo*

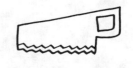

saw *el serrucho*

screwdriver *el destornillador*

90

Are you still coloring? Circle the word that fits the sentence:

(La escalera, la flor, la oveja) es un animal.

(El serrucho, la tortuga, el árbol) es una herramienta.

(El rastrillo, el arbusto, la vaca) es una planta.

ANSWERS: *la oveja, el serrucho, el arbusto*

Now, connect the words that belong together:

las hojas	*el martillo*
la tierra	*la escoba*
el piso	*el rastrillo*
el clavo	*la manguera*
el agua	*la pala*

ANSWERS: *las hojas* — *el rastrillo*; *la tierra* — *la pala*; *el piso* — *la escoba*; *el clavo* — *el martillo*; *el agua* — *la manguera*

Cross out every other letter and read the secret message:

M o e t g o u p s í t r a s m ó i f j m a n r e d o í o n a .

ANSWERS: *Me gusta mi jardín.* (I like my garden.)

¡Vamos!
(Let's go!)

When you are finished in the garden, ask someone to give you a ride around town. SPANISH is everywhere, so get ready to learn a lot.

Look at the . . . *Mira* . . .

car   **el carro**
subway   **el metro**

truck   **el camión**

motorcycle   *la motocicleta*

bus   **el autobús**

Choose the best word from the list above:

Students take this to school.   _____

Only one police officer can ride on it.   _____

This thing goes underground.   _____

ANSWERS: el autobús, la motocicleta, el metro

Which one is bigger?

el camión o la motocicleta
el carro o el metro
el autobús o la bicicleta

ANSWERS: el camión, el metro, el autobús

These can carry people, too:

submarine   *el submarino*
boat   *el bote*
train   *el tren*

ship
el barco

plane
el avión

Fill in the missing letters, and then write the English:

e l   _ a _ _ o

_____

l a   _ o t _ _ i c _ _ t a

_____

e l   _ u _ o b _ s

_____

e l   t _ e _

_____

e l   a _ i _ n

_____

e l   _ _ t r _

_____

Now, connect the sentences that mean the same:

Vamos en el barco.   Bring the new car.

Los taxis son amarillos.   They are on the train.

Trae el carro nuevo.   I like the truck.

Me gusta el camión.   Let's go in the ship.

Están en el tren.   The taxis are yellow.

ANSWERS: *Vamos en el barco.* Let's go in the ship. / *Los taxis son amarillos.* The taxis are yellow. / *Trae el carro nuevo.* Bring the new car. / *Me gusta el camión.* I like the truck. / *Están en el tren.* They are on the train.

Can you ask these questions in SPANISH?

Where is the car?
What color is the car?
Do you like the car?

ANSWERS: *¿Dónde está el carro?* / *¿De qué color es el carro?* / *¿Te gusta el carro?*

La ciudad
(The City)

Look out the window as you go downtown.
When you see something, say it in SPANISH:

street   *la calle*
sidewalk   *la acera*
mailbox   *el buzón*

building *el edificio*

traffic light
el semáforo

fence *la cerca*

sign *el letrero*

bridge *el puente*

Keep pointing:

Point to the. . . *Señala . . .*

bank   *el banco*
church   *la iglesia*
school   *la escuela*

restaurant *el restaurante*

store *la tienda*

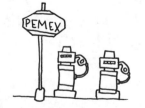

gas station *la gasolinera*

O.K. Answer these questions in SPANISH:

Where do people keep their money?   *En el banco*

Where do people buy their clothing?   _____

Where do people go out to eat?   _____

Where do people get gas for their cars?   _____

What do these sentences mean?

Vamos al buzón.   _____ .

Vamos a la iglesia.   _____ .

Vamos al puente.   _____ .

A EL =AL
DE EL = DEL

Al y Del
("To the" and "Of the")

Spanish people got tired of saying *a el* and *de el* so they shortened them to *al* and *del*. Look:

Let's go <u>to the</u> mailbox.   *Vamos <u>al</u> buzón.*
It's in front <u>of the</u> building.   *Está enfrente <u>del</u> edificio.*

If you visit the city, use words that tell "where."
Put any of these on the lines below:

detrás　　*cerca*　　*enfrente*　　*lejos*

El letrero está _____ *del restaurante.*

La cerca está _____ *de la escuela.*

El semáforo está _____ *de la calle.*

Connect each picture below with the correct word.
Then, add <u>color</u> to everything!

la flor　　*el semáforo*　　*el pájaro*　　*el edificio*　　*el puente*

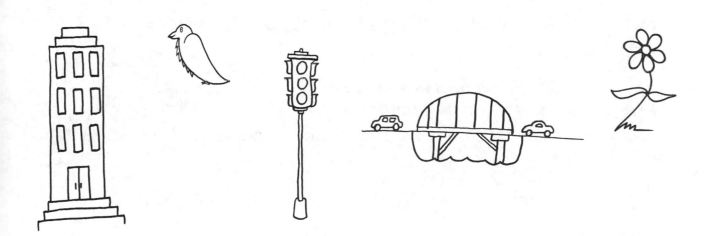

La gente
(People)

The city is a busy place. Wave to each person you see:

nurse **el enfermero**
firefighter **el bombero**
mechanic **el mecánico**
salesperson **el vendedor**

student **el estudiante**

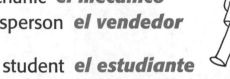

teacher
el maestro

doctor **el doctor**

police officer **el policía**

Don't forget! Most words that describe girls end in the letter **a**:

**María es una mecánica y
Susana es una enfermera.**
Mary is a mechanic and Susan is a nurse.

Read this story aloud. What does it mean in English?

Mi madre es una doctora. Ella es muy inteligente. No está en la casa hoy. Está en el hospital. Mi padre es un vendedor y es muy chistoso. Es un vendedor de zapatos. No está en su tienda hoy. Él está en la casa.

ANSWER: My mother is a doctor. She is very smart. She is not at home today. She is at the hospital. My father is a salesman. He is very funny. He is a shoe salesman. He is not at his store today. He is at home.

Cross out the word that does not fit:

tienda, banco, restaurante, buzón

caballo, metro, vaca, oveja

vendedor, maestro, martillo, bombero

mecánico, avión, barco, autobús

semáforo, calle, edificio, piedra

ANSWERS: *buzón, metro, martillo, mecánico, piedra*

Más trabajadores
(More Workers)

pilot	*el piloto*
dentist	*el dentista*
secretary	*el secretario*

waiter *el mesero*

mail carrier
el cartero

cook *el cocinero*

Circle the words that look a lot like English:

el dentista   *el mesero*   *el cartero*   *el doctor*

el bombero   *el piloto*   *el vendedor*   *el cocinero*

ANSWERS: *el dentista, el doctor, el piloto*

Connect the beginning of each sentence with its correct ending:

El cartero está	*en el hospital.*
El piloto está	*en el garaje.*
El cocinero está	*en la calle.*
La doctora está	*en el avión.*
El mecánico está	*en el restaurante.*

Try these questions with friends and their families
who speak only SPANISH:

Do you work?	*¿Trabajas?*
Where do you work?	*¿Dónde trabajas?*
Do you like your job?	*¿Te gusta tu trabajo?*

Write three words under each category:

City Buildings	Workers	Transportation
_____	_____	_____
_____	_____	_____
_____	_____	_____

¿Quién eres tú?
(Who are you?)

Use the word *Soy* to talk about yourself in SPANISH:

I'm Tina.	*Soy Tina.*
I'm a student.	*Soy estudiante.*
I'm smart.	*Soy inteligente.*

Can you tell what these people are saying?

Soy el Sr. López.   I'm Mr. Lopez.

Soy bombero.   _____ .

Soy muy fuerte.   _____ .

Soy la Sra. González.   I'm Mrs. González.

Soy maestra.   _____ .

Soy de Cuba.   _____ .

Soy Linda.   _____ .

Soy esposa y madre.   _____ .

Soy alta y bonita.   _____ .

ANSWERS: I'm a firefighter. I'm very strong.
I'm a teacher. I'm from Cuba.
I'm Linda. I'm a wife and mother. I'm tall and pretty.

And what about you? *¿Quién eres tú?*

Soy _____ . *Soy* _____ . *Soy* _____ .

¡Mira! You can say a lot about yourself in SPANISH.
Read these words aloud:

I'm very happy.	*Estoy muy feliz.*
I'm a student of SPANISH.	*Soy estudiante de español.*
I understand a lot of SPANISH.	*Entiendo mucho español.*
I like SPANISH a lot.	*Me gusta mucho el español.*
I want more SPANISH!	*¡Quiero más español!*

Match each question with its answer:

¿Cuándo trabajas?	*Su nombre es Ana.*
¿Eres un maestro?	*Sí, estoy aquí.*
¿Quién es la vendedora?	*Tres.*
¿Estás en la tienda?	*No, soy piloto.*
¿Cuántos policías hay?	*Mañana.*

Try out this conversation with a friend:

#1 *¿Quién eres tú?*
#2 *Soy policía. ¿Qué quieres?*
#1 *¿Dónde está la tienda de juguetes?*
#2 *Está allí, enfrente del edificio grande.*
#1 *¿Está cerca de la gasolinera?*
#2 *Sí. El letrero es blanco y azul.*
#1 *¡Fantástico! Muchas gracias.*
#2 *De nada. Adiós.*

ANSWERS:
#1 Who are you?
#2 I'm a police officer. What do you want?
#1 Where is the toy store?
#2 It's there, in front of the big building.
#1 Is it near the gas station?
#2 Yes. The sign is white and blue.
#1 Great! Thanks a lot.
#2 You're welcome. Good-bye.

This time, put the letters in numerical order.
Find out where we're going in the next chapter:

M (3)   *L* (7)   *S* (10)   *V* (1)   *A* (15)   *E* (13)   *C* (11)   *A* (6)
O (4)   *A* (2)   *E* (9)   *U* (12)   *A* (8)   *S* (5)   *L* (14)

ANSWER: *Vamos a la escuela.*

Did you finish all the questions and puzzles
in this chapter? *¡Qué bueno!* Now you
can turn the page, go to school, and
speak more SPANISH every day!

6 CHAPTER
SEIS

En la escuela

(At School)

Mi escuela
(My School)

Speak SPANISH on your way to school. And when you get there, name whatever you see!

Look at the teachers and students.
Mira los maestros y los estudiantes.

Let's go to the . . .   *Vamos a . . .*

flag	*la bandera*
office	*la oficina*
benches	*los bancos*
classroom	*el salón de clase*
blackboard	*el pizarrón*
playground	*el campo de recreo*

Study this map. Write the word that matches each number you find:

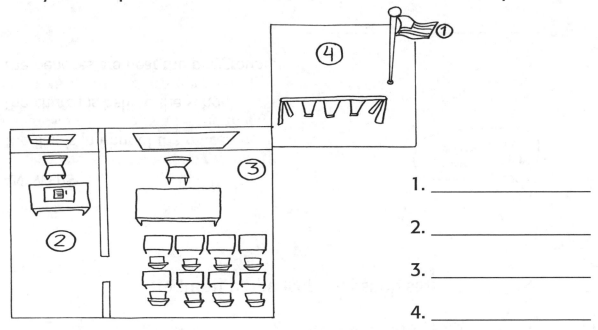

1. _____

2. _____

3. _____

4. _____

ANSWERS: 1. *la bandera* 2. *la oficina* 3. *el salón de clase* 4. *el campo de recreo*

Write these "backward" sentences correctly. Then, put what they mean in English:

.anicifo al ed etnerfne átse arednab aL

SPANISH: _____

ENGLISH: _____

.aleucse al ed sárted átse aiselgi aL

SPANISH: _____

ENGLISH: _____

.oercer ed opmac led acrec nátse socnab soL

SPANISH: _____

ENGLISH: _____

ANSWERS:

La bandera está enfrente de la oficina.
The flag is in front of the office.
La iglesia está detrás de la escuela.
The church is behind the school.
Los bancos están cerca del campo de recreo.
The benches are near the playground.

Estoy en el grado cuatro.

Try this question. Just add a number:

What grade are you in?   *¿En qué grado estás?*

I'm in <u>fourth</u> grade.   *Estoy en el grado <u>cuatro</u>.*

Now, remember all the SPANISH words you have learned, and use them to write about yourself:

_____

_____

_____

_____

Mi salón de clase
(My Classroom)

Be very quiet as you practice in the classroom. Look at these things and say their name in SPANISH:

desk *el escritorio*

pencil sharpener
el sacapuntas

bulletin board
el tablero de anuncios

map *el mapa*   bell *la campana*

Unscramble these letters now:

oirtseocri   *tusaacanps*   *maapacn*

_____   _____   _____

Name everything in this backpack. "Backpack" is called *la mochila* in SPANISH.

paper	*el papel*
pencil	*el lápiz*
pen	*el lapicero*
eraser	*el borrador*
notebook	*el cuaderno*

This time, connect each word with its meaning:

blackboard	*el papel*
pencil	*el cuaderno*
paper	*el lápiz*
desk	*el escritorio*
notebook	*el pizarrón*

ANSWERS:
blackboard *el pizarrón*
pencil *el lápiz*
paper *el papel*
desk *el escritorio*
notebook *el cuaderno*

Circle the word that doesn't belong:

el lápiz, el lapicero, el banco

la bandera, la maestra, el estudiante

el papel, la campana, el cuaderno

ANSWERS: *el banco, la bandera, la campana*

¿Qué necesitas?
(What do you need?)

Tell everyone what you need in SPANISH:

I need the . . .   *Necesito . . .*

crayons *los gises*

chalk *la tiza*

scissors *las tijeras*

glue *el pegamento*

marker *el marcador*

Connect each picture with the proper word:

las tijeras   *los gises*   *el pegamento*   *el marcador*

Now, fill in the blank with the correct word:

la pelota   el papel   el almuerzo

Tengo hambre. Necesito _____ .

¿Dónde están mis juguetes? Necesito _____ .

Quiero mi cuaderno. Necesito _____ .

ANSWERS: el almuerzo, la pelota, el papel

You learned these words before, but do you remember them?
Write what they mean in English:

la computadora _____

el reloj _____

el libro _____

el bote de basura _____

el gabinete _____

Put **T** for true and **F** for false:

Los estudiantes están en los escritorios. _____

El pizarrón está en el campo de recreo. _____

Los papeles están en la bandera. _____

El libro está en el salón de clase. _____

Los bancos están en el sacapuntas. _____

¡Lo tengo!
(I have it!)

Tell others what you have in SPANISH:

Do you have your pencil? **¿Tienes tu lápiz?**
Yes, I have it! **¡Sí, lo tengo!**

Do you have your paper? **¿Tienes tu papel?**
No, I don't have it! **¡No, no lo tengo!**

Do you have your ____? **¿Tienes tu ____ ?**

The word **tiene** means "has" in SPANISH.

The school has a big office.
La escuela tiene una oficina grande.

The teacher has the scissors and crayons.
El maestro tiene las tijeras y los gises.

My classroom has _____.

Mi salón de clase tiene _____ .

Put the correct word on the lines below:

tiene   tienes   tengo

¿Tú _____ tu libro?

Yo no _____ mi cuaderno.

Ella _____ su lápiz y borrador.

ANSWERS: *tienes, tengo, tiene*

111

¡De es muy necesario!
(De is very necessary!)

When something belongs to someone, use the word *de*:

It is Victor's pencil.   *Es el lápiz de Víctor.*
It is the teacher's desk.   *Es el escritorio del maestro.*

Try some:

It's Mary's book.   _____

It's Joe's pen.   _____

Mi clase favorita
(My Favorite Class)

You can learn many things at school. What do you like best?

I like . . .   *Me gusta . . .*

music   *la música*
math   *las matemáticas*
art   *el arte*
social studies   *los estudios sociales*
science   *la ciencia*
language   *el lenguaje*

Which of these words go together?

las pinturas   *la ciencia*

los números   *el lenguaje*

el radio   *el arte*

los animales   *las matemáticas*

el español   *la música*

El mundo grande
(The Big World)

Let's learn about
the world.
Use a map
to practice:

state   *el estado*

country   *el país*

world   *el mundo*

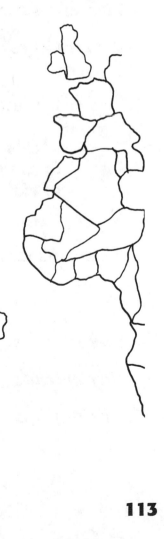

113

Look at the . . .   *Mira . . .*

desert   *el desierto*
lake   *el lago*

forest   *el bosque*

mountain   *la montaña*

river   *el río*

Did you color everything?   *¡Muy bien!*   Now say where you live:

Vivo en la calle _____ (your street)

Vivo en la ciudad de _____ (your town)

Vivo en el estado de _____ (your state)

Join the words that go together . . .

el desierto   *alta*
la montaña   *azul*
el río   *calor*

ANSWERS: *el desierto   calor*
la montaña   alta
el río   azul

. . . and fill in the blank:

botes   estados   árboles

Hay muchos _____ *en el bosque.*

Hay muchos _____ *en el lago.*

Hay muchos _____ *en el país.*

ANSWERS: *Hay muchos árboles en el bosque.*
Hay muchos botes en el lago.
Hay muchos estados en el país.

114

So, how much SPANISH do you think you know? Let's see! Write what these words mean in English:

Mi país tiene cincuenta estados.   _____

Mira los dos lagos bonitos.   _____

Los tigres están en el bosque.   _____

Hace frío en las montañas.   _____

El desierto está cerca de aquí.   _____

El campo de recreo
(The Playground)

After school, tell the SPANISH names of these fun things:

Let's go to the . . .   *Vamos a . . .*

merry-go-round   *los caballitos*
bars   *las barras*

seesaw *el subibaja*

swing *el columpio*

slide *el resbalador*

Fill in the missing letters:

el __ e __ __ a l __ __ o __   *el __ o __ u __ p __ o*

el __ __ b i __ a __ __

You learned about these things earlier. Write in the English:

Trae . . .	Bring the . . .
el bate	<u>bat</u>
la pelota	_____
el guante	_____

la bicicleta	_____
la patineta	_____
el juguete	_____

¡Dame!
(Give me!)

Here's a <u>new</u> command. Use *Dame* to say "Give me":

Give me the ball!	*¡Dame la pelota!*
Give me the toy!	_____
Give me the skateboard!	_____

116

Los juegos
(The Games)

How do you have fun **en español**?

basketball **el baloncesto**   soccer **el fútbol**
baseball **el béisbol**
drawing **el dibujo**

reading **la lectura**

dancing **el baile**

Put one of these words on the lines below:

I like _____ a lot.   **Me gusta _____ mucho.**

Do you like _____ ?   **¿Te gusta _____ ?**

Match the words that go together:

los gises   **la lectura**
la pelota   **el dibujo**
el libro   **el béisbol**

Put the words in each sentence in the right order:

juego   fútbol   Es   de   un.
dibujo   clase   de   la   Vamos   a.
blanco   Yo   un   tengo   béisbol.

117

Write three words under each category:

El salón de clase

_____

_____

_____

El campo de recreo

_____

_____

_____

¡Usted y Tú!
("You" and "You!")

Say **usted** to your teacher instead of **tú**.
Use **tú** only with your family and friends:

| How are <u>you</u>, my friend? | **¿Cómo estás <u>tú</u>, mi amigo?** |
| How are <u>you</u>, teacher? | **¿Cómo está <u>usted</u>, maestro?** |

Más diversión
(More Fun)

| stories | **los cuentos** | songs | **las canciones** |
| tricks | **los trucos** | | |

cartoons
los dibujos animados

los chistes
jokes

Let's go to the . . .   *Vamos a . . .*

park *el parque*

movies *el cine*

zoo *el zoológico*

Answer these questions by writing in SPANISH:

los chistes   los dibujos animados   los trucos

What does a magician do? _____

What do you call funny stories? _____

What do you watch on TV? _____

ANSWERS: *los trucos, los chistes, los dibujos animados*

Which words belong together?

la música   el parque
los árboles   el zoológico
los leones   la canción

ANSWERS: *la música   la canción*
los árboles   el parque
los leones   el zoológico

Look at this CROSSWORD puzzle. Put these words in SPANISH:

ACROSS
2. songs
3. country
4. reading
5. forest

DOWN
1. desert
2. movies
3. park

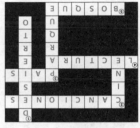

ANSWERS:

Celebremos
(Let's Celebrate)

There are many special days during the year. Here are a few in SPANISH:

Happy Birthday!	*¡Feliz cumpleaños!*
Merry Christmas!	*¡Feliz Navidad!*
Happy Easter!	*¡Felices Pascuas!*

I want the . . .	*Quiero . . .*
party	*la fiesta*
cake	*la torta*
present	*el regalo*

candy *los dulces*

ice cream *el helado*

candles *las velas*

Can you remember what you learned?
Write these party words in English:

los juegos y los globos _____

mi familia y mis amigos _____

la música y el baile _____

ANSWERS: the games and the balloons
my family and my friends
the music and the dancing

Answer these questions in SPANISH:

¿Cuántas velas hay en la torta? _____

¿Cuántos regalos hay en la mesa? _____

¿Cuántos globos hay en la fiesta? _____

ANSWERS: *diez, cinco, siete*

121

Try this conversation. But first, say what it means in English:

#1 *Hoy es mi cumpleaños.*
#2 *¡Qué bueno! ¿Cuántos años tienes?*
#1 *Tengo once. Estoy muy feliz.*
#2 *¿Hay una fiesta en tu casa?*
#1 *Sí, y vamos al cine en la noche.*

Name all your favorite snacks:

Bring . . .   *Trae . . .*
Give me . . .   *Dame . . .*
Take . . .   *Toma . . .*

pie *el pastel*

jello   *la gelatina*
cookies   *las galletas*

gum *el chicle*

popcorn *las palomitas*

122

Connect the words that belong together:

el helado   las palomitas
la música   el frío
la torta   la gelatina
el maíz   el baile
la fresa   las velas

Underline only the things you can eat:

los dulces   los cumpleaños   los regalos

las galletas   los pasteles   los globos

Match each picture with the correct word:

el pastel

las galletas

los regalos

la torta

las palomitas

Say these things in SPANISH at your next party:

Welcome!   *¡Bienvenido!*
Congratulations!   *¡Felicitaciones!*
Good luck!   *¡Buena suerte!*

I hope you had fun today. Now, let's hurry home.
Are you speaking SPANISH every day?

7 CHAPTER
SIETE

De noche

(At Night)

Mucha ayuda
(A Lot of Help)

After you get home from school, help around the house.
Begin by setting the table for dinner.

Do you need help?   *¿Necesitas ayuda?*
Yes, I need the . . .   *Sí, necesito . . .*

plate *el plato*

glass *el vaso*

napkin *la servilleta*

cup *la taza*

bowl *el plato hondo*

saucer *el platillo*

fork *el tenedor*

spoon *la cuchara*

knife *el cuchillo*

Connect the words that go together:

la taza   *el tenedor*
la silla   *el platillo*
la cuchara   *la mesa*

ANSWERS: la taza   el platillo
la silla   la mesa
la cuchara   el tenedor

126

Put the word that belongs on the line:

el cuchillo   *el vaso*   *el plato hondo*

Quiero _____ *de leche.*

La sopa está en _____ .

No tengo el tenedor, _____ , *y la cuchara.*

Whenever you help, add a SPANISH word to each command:

Bring . . .   *Trae . . .* _____

Give me . . .   *Dame . . .* _____

Take . . .   *Toma . . .* _____

> Trae.
> Dame.

Here's a <u>new</u> one.   Fill in the blanks:

> Toma.
> Pon.

Put . . .   *Pon . . .* _____

Put the napkins there.   *Pon las servilletas allí.*

Put the cup on the saucer.   _____ .

Put the spoon in the bowl.   _____ .

Now, connect the sentences that mean the same:

Let's go to the kitchen.	*Mira las tazas nuevas.*
Put the fork here.	*Me gusta la servilleta roja.*
There are six big plates.	*No tienes un plato hondo.*
The glass is on the table.	*Vamos a la cocina.*
Look at the new cups.	*El vaso está en la mesa.*
I like the red napkin.	*Pon el tenedor aquí.*
You don't have a bowl.	*Hay seis platos grandes.*

ANSWERS: Let's go to the kitchen. *Vamos a la cocina.*
Put the fork here. *Pon el tenedor aquí.*
There are six big plates. *Hay seis platos grandes.*
The glass is on the table. *El vaso está en la mesa.*
Look at the new cups. *Mira las tazas nuevas.*
I like the red napkin. *Me gusta la servilleta roja.*
You don't have a bowl. *No tienes un plato hondo.*

¡La limpieza!
(Cleanup!)

After dinner, start cleaning around the house:

I need the . . .	*Necesito . . .*
towel	*la toalla*
soap	*el jabón*

mop *el trapeador*

bucket *el balde*

sponge *la esponja*

128

Clean up with words you know. Write the English:

el agua ____________________

la escoba ____________________

el bote de basura ____________________

ANSWERS: water, broom, trash can

Connect each question with the best answer:

¿Dónde está el agua?	***En el bote de basura.***
¿Dónde está el papel?	***En la lavadora.***
¿Dónde está la toalla?	***En el balde.***

ANSWERS: *¿Dónde está el agua?* *En el balde.*
¿Dónde está el papel? *En el bote de basura.*
¿Dónde está la toalla? *En la lavadora.*

Write the word to match each picture below:

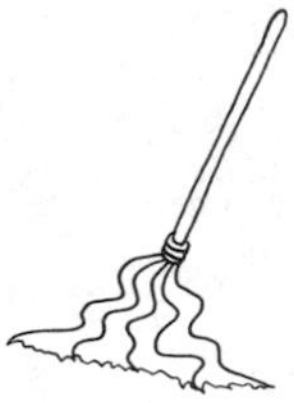
1. ________________

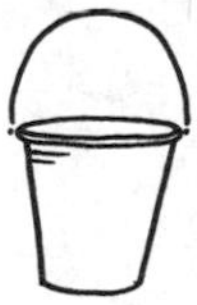
2. ________________

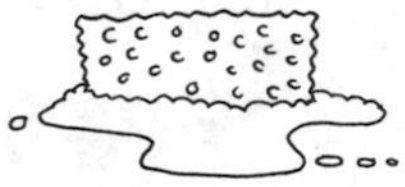
3. ________________

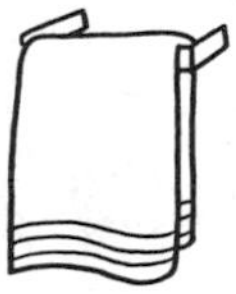
4. ________________

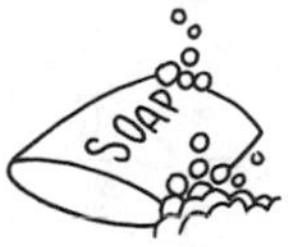

5. ________________

ANSWERS: 1. el trapeador 2. el balde 3. la esponja 4. la toalla 5. el jabón

This new command makes cleaning easy. Can you fill in the blanks?

Clean the . . .	*Limpia . . .*
house	*la* _ _ _ _
room	*el* _ _ _ _ _ _
table	*la* _ _ _ _

Choose the right answer:

el trapeador   **la esponja**   **la escoba**

Hay tierra en la calle. Trae _____ .

Hay agua en el piso. Trae _____ .

Hay comida en la silla. Trae _____ .

Here are more things you can say:

It's clean.	*Está limpia.*
It's dirty.	*Está sucia.*

What do these words mean?

¿Dónde está la toalla limpia? _____

Tengo los zapatos sucios. _____

Mi ropero está muy limpio. _____

130

Which cleaning tools always go together?
Break this code to find the answer:

1 2 3 4 5 6 7 8 9 10 11 12 13 14 15 16 17 18 19 20 21 22 23 24 25
A B C D E F G H I J K L M N O P Q R S T U V W X Y

5-12   2-1-12-4-5   25   5-12   20-18-1-16-5-1-4-15-18

El baño
(The Bathroom)

Cleaning the house can be dirty work. Get washed up in the bathroom:

mirror
el espejo

toilet
el excusado

shower
la ducha

sink *el lavabo*

faucet *el grifo*

bathtub *la tina*

You know these bathroom words. Write them in SPANISH:

I like the water.　　　　*Me gusta* _____ .

I like the towel.　　　　_____ .

I like the soap.　　　　_____ .

Cross out the word that doesn't belong:

la tina, la ducha, la escuela
el grifo, el tren, el lavabo
el cuchillo, el agua, el jabón

ANSWERS: *la escuela, el tren, el cuchillo*

Speak SPANISH when you turn on the water:

It's hot.	*Está caliente.*
It's cold.	*Está fría.*

Color this funny picture. Then, fill in the blanks:

encima del excusado	*en la ducha*	*enfrente del espejo*

El perro está _____ .

El caballo está _____ .

El gato está _____ .

ANSWERS: *El perro está enfrente del espejo.*
El caballo está en la ducha.
El gato está encima del excusado.

Put the words in these sentences in order, and write
what they mean in English:

mira baño la al y ducha Anda _____

lavabo Pon caliente el en agua el _____

la Toma y tina limpia esponja la _____

Take the sponge and clean the bathtub.
Put hot water in the sink.
Go to the bathroom and look at the shower.

ANSWERS:
Anda al baño y mira la ducha.
Pon el agua caliente en el lavabo.
Toma la esponja y limpia la tina.

O.K. Go into the bathroom, and point:

Point to the . . . *Señala . . .*

hairbrush *el cepillo*

comb *el peine*

toothbrush *el cepillo de dientes*

toothpaste
la pasta de dientes

Underline the correct word:

Mi peine es (guapo, viejo, osito).

Pon el cepillo en el (libro, metro, baño).

El lavabo tiene un (grifo, gato, zapato).

La pasta de dientes es (camisa, alto, verde).

El espejo está (limpio, feliz, caliente).

ANSWERS: *viejo, baño, grifo, verde, limpio*

Mi cuerpo
(My Body)

As long as you are in the bathroom, why not take a bath in SPANISH!
Say each part as you scrub:

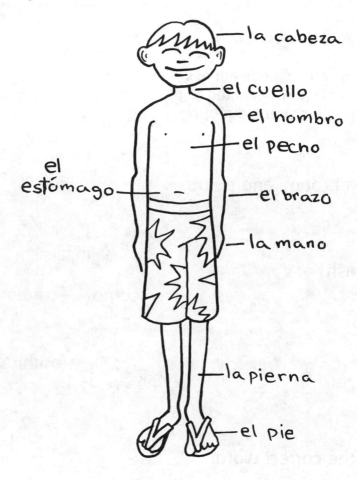

- la cabeza
- el cuello
- el hombro
- el pecho
- el estómago
- el brazo
- la mano
- la pierna
- el pie

The command word for "Wash" is **_Lava_**. Write three things that can be washed on the lines below:

Lava _____

Lava _____

Lava _____

Put these letters in order:

m o h o r b   _____

r i n e a p   _____

ó g o t e m s a   _____

z a a c e b   _____

l o c u l e   _____

h o p e c   _____

ANSWERS: *hombro, pierna, estómago, cabeza, cuello, pecho*

Connect the dots. What do you see—in SPANISH?

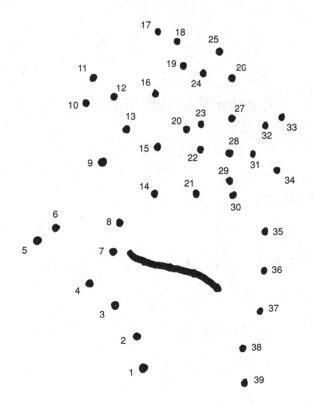

ANSWERS: *La mano*

135

La cara
(The Face)

Every time you look into the mirror, speak SPANISH:

Look at the . . .   *Mira . . .*

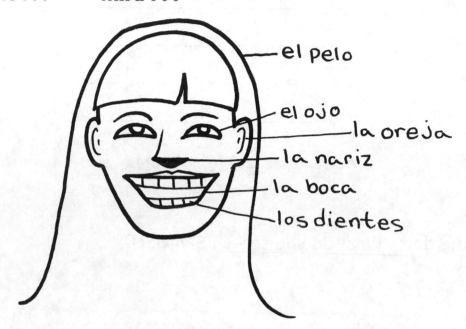

el pelo

el ojo

la oreja

la nariz

la boca

los dientes

Read these words as you color the girl's face:

Los ojos son azules.
El pelo es café.
Los dientes son blancos.

Here are two different monsters. What do they look
like in SPANISH?

It has three eyes.   <u>*Tiene tres ojos.*</u>

It has two heads.   _____ .

It has four arms.   _____ .

There are four ears.   **_Hay cuatro orejas._**

There are three legs.   _____ .

There are five teeth.   _____ .

Now draw this monster:

Tiene dos bocas, una nariz grande, y mucho pelo verde:

Estoy enfermo
(I'm sick)

Talk in SPANISH when you don't feel well:

I need the . . .   *Necesito . . .*

aspirin   *la aspirina*
vitamin   *la vitamina*

 medicine
la medicina

Band-aid
la curita

thermometer *el termómetro*

Circle the three words that look a lot like English:

enfermo   vitamina   curita   medicina   aspirina

¿Qué te pasa? means "What's the matter?"

It's a . . .   *Es . . .*

cough   *la tos*
cold   *el resfriado*
fever   *la fiebre*

 I have a . . .   *Tengo un . . .*

stomachache   *dolor de estómago*
headache   *dolor de cabeza*
toothache   *dolor de muela*

Connect the words that belong together:

dolor de cabeza   *el dentista*
dolor de estómago *la aspirina*
dolor de muela   *la comida*

Practice, and then write these words in English:

#1 *¿Qué te pasa? ¿Estás enfermo?*

_____

#2 *Sí. Tengo dolor de cabeza y fiebre.*

_____

#1 *¿Quieres un doctor?*

_____

#2 *No, gracias. Necesito un termómetro y aspirina.*

_____

139

A la cama
(Off to Bed)

It's bedtime, so . . . *anda a la cama.*

Are you all tucked in? *¡Muy bien!* Now, look out the window and talk about the sky at night:

Look at the . . .   *Mira . . .*

star	*la estrella*
moon	*la luna*
rocket	*el cohete*
space	*el espacio*

planet
el planeta

comet *el cometa*

Put different words on the lines below. Then, read in SPANISH:

Señala _____ .

Me gusta _____ .

Vamos a _____ .

Color these things:

Tres planetas verdes, cafés y azules

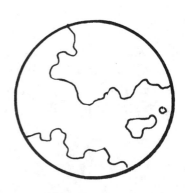 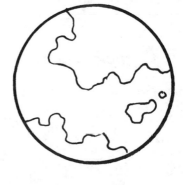 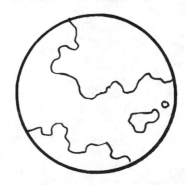

Una estrella amarilla

Dos cohetes rojos

Dime un cuento
(Tell me a story)

Before you fall asleep, take out your favorite storybook.
Name these characters *en español*:

It is the . . .   *Es . . .*

wizard *el mago*

princess   *la princesa*
fairy   *la hada*

king *el rey*

elf *el duende*

Here is the . . .   *Aquí tienes . . .*

ghost   *el fantasma*
giant   *el gigante*

witch
la bruja

monster
el monstruo

dragon
el dragón

Answer with **T** for TRUE and **F** for FALSE:

El duende es más grande que el gigante.   _____

La hija del rey es la princesa.   _____

Las brujas son muy bonitas.   _____

ANSWERS: F, T, F

There is a secret character hidden below. Circle every other letter to find out who it is:

O S T O L Y O C A H S I A C M O O Y I T

T E N N E G R O S L K A O S B O A R F E

O J O A L S I G A R N A S N O D E E P S

What's the secret message?   _____

Which character am I?   _____

ANSWERS: *Soy chico y tengo las orejas grandes. (¡Soy un duende!)*
I am small and I have big ears. (I'm an elf!)

142

Draw a line from these words to each picture:

La bruja tiene su escoba.

La princesa está muy triste.

El fantasma está en la casa.

Soon it will be morning. When you wake up, turn to Chapter One, and read this book again!

Hablo español
(I Speak Spanish)

Have you learned all the words in this book?

¡Qué bueno!

Now—from the time you get up until
the time you go to bed—
you can really speak . . .

. . . SPANISH every day!

VOCABULARY LIST

ENGLISH	ESPAÑOL
a	*un* or *una*
a little	*poca* or *poco*
a lot	*mucha* or *mucho*
above	*encima*
address	*la dirección*
after	*después*
all	*toda* or *todo*
almost	*casi*
always	*siempre*
American	*americana* or *americano*
an	*un* or *una*
and	*y*
angel	*el ángel*
angry	*enojada* or *enojado*
animal	*el animal*
another	*otra* or *otro*
ant	*la hormiga*
apartment	*el apartamento*
apple	*la manzana*
April	*abril*
arm	*el brazo*
armchair	*el sillón*
art	*el arte*
aspirin	*la aspirina*
astronaut	*el astronauta*
at	*en*
attic	*el desván*
August	*agosto*

aunt	*la tía*
baby	*el bebé*
back	*la espalda*
backpack	*la mochila*
bad	*mala* or *malo*
bag	*la bolsa*
ball	*la pelota*
balloon	*el globo*
banana	*el plátano*
Band-aid	*la curita*
bank	*el banco*
bars	*las barras*
baseball	*el béisbol*
basement	*el sótano*
basketball	*el baloncesto*
bat	*el bate*
bathroom	*el baño*
bathtub	*la tina*
beach	*la playa*
beans	*los frijoles*
bed	*la cama*
bedroom	*el dormitorio*
bedspread	*la cubrecama*
bee	*la abeja*
before	*antes*
behind	*detrás*
bell	*la campana*
belt	*el cinturón*
benches	*los bancos*
bicycle	*la bicicleta*
big	*grande*
bird	*el pájaro*
black	*negra* or *negro*
blackboard	*el pizarrón*
blanket	*la frazada*
blocks	*los bloques*
blouse	*la blusa*
blue	*azul*

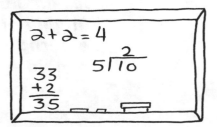

145

body	*el cuerpo*
book	*el libro*
bookshelf	*el librero*
boots	*las botas*
bottle	*la botella*
bowl	*el plato hondo*
boy	*el niño*
bracelet	*el brazalete*
brave	*valiente*
bread	*el pan*
breakfast	*el desayuno*
bridge	*el puente*
broom	*la escoba*
brother	*el hermano*
brown	*café*
bucket	*el balde*
building	*el edificio*
bulletin board	*el tablero de anuncios*
bus	*el autobús*
bush	*el arbusto*
but	*pero*
butter	*la mantequilla*
cabinet	*el gabinete*
cake	*la torta*
calendar	*el calendario*
camera	*la cámara*
candles	*las velas*
candy	*los dulces*
cap	*la gorra*
car	*el carro*
carpet	*la alfombra*
carrot	*la zanahoria*
cartoons	*los dibujos animados*
cat	*la gata* or *el gato*
ceiling	*el techo*
celery	*el apio*

chair	*la silla*
chalk	*la tiza*
chapter	*el capítulo*
cheap	*barata* or *barato*
checkers	*el juego de damas*
cheese	*el queso*
chest	*el pecho*
chicken	*el pollo*
children	*los niños*
chimney	*la chimenea*
chocolate	*el chocolate*
church	*la iglesia*
city	*la ciudad*
class	*la clase*
classroom	*el salón de clase*
clean	*limpia* or *limpio*
clock	*el reloj*
closed	*cerrada* or *cerrado*
closet	*el ropero*
clothes	*la ropa*
cloudy	*nublada* or *nublado*
clown	*el payaso*
coffee	*el café*
coin	*la moneda*
cold (flu)	*el resfriado*
cold (temperature)	*fría* or *frío*
color	*el color*
comb	*el peine*
comet	*el cometa*
computer	*la computadora*
cook	*el cocinero*
cookies	*las galletas*
corn	*el maíz*
corner	*la esquina*
couch	*el sofá*
cough	*la tos*
country	*el país*

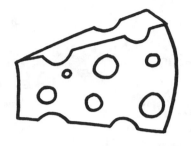

cousin	*la prima* or *el primo*
cow	*la vaca*
crayons	*los gises*
crazy	*loca* or *loco*
cup	*la taza*
curtains	*las cortinas*
dancing	*el baile*
dangerous	*peligrosa* or *peligroso*
dark	*oscura* or *oscuro*
daughter	*la hija*
day	*el día*
December	*diciembre*
deer	*el venado*
dentist	*la* or *el dentista*
desert	*el desierto*
desk	*el escritorio*
dessert	*el postre*
different	*diferente*
difficult	*difícil*
dining room	*el comedor*
dinner	*la cena*
dinosaur	*el dinosaurio*
dirt	*la tierra*
dirty	*sucia* or *sucio*
dishes	*la loza*
doctor	*la doctora* or *el doctor*
dog	*la perra* or *el perro*
doll	*la muñeca*
dollar	*el dólar*
donkey	*la burra* or *el burro*
door	*la puerta*
down	*abajo*
dragon	*el dragón*
drawing	*el dibujo*
dress	*el vestido*
dresser	*el tocador*
drinks	*las bebidas*

drum	*el tambor*
dry	*seca* or *seco*
dryer	*la secadora*
duck	*la pata* or *el pato*
each	*cada*
ear	*la oreja*
early	*temprano*
earrings	*los aretes*
easy	*fácil*
egg	*el huevo*
eight	*ocho*
eighteen	*dieciocho*
eighty	*ochenta*
elephant	*la elefanta* or *el elefante*
elevator	*el ascensor*
eleven	*once*
elf	*el duende*
empty	*vacía* or *vacío*
end	*el fin*
engine	*el motor*
English	*el inglés*
enough	*bastante*
envelope	*el sobre*
eraser	*el borrador*
everybody	*todas* or *todos*
excellent	*excelente*
excited	*emocionada* or *emocionado*
expensive	*cara* or *caro*
eye	*el ojo*
face	*la cara*
factory	*la fábrica*
fairy	*la hada*
fall	*el otoño*
family	*la familia*
fantastic	*fantástica* or *fantástico*
far	*lejos*
farm	*la finca*

fat	*gorda* or *gordo*
father	*el padre*
fast	*rápida* or *rápido*
faucet	*el grifo*
favorite	*favorita* or *favorito*
feather	*la pluma*
February	*febrero*
fence	*la cerca*
fever	*la fiebre*
few	*poca* or *poco*
fifteen	*quince*
fifty	*cincuenta*
fine	*bien*
firefighter	*el bombero*
first	*primera* or *primero*
fish	*el pescado*
five	*cinco*
flag	*la bandera*
floor	*el piso*
flower	*la flor*
fly	*la mosca*
food	*la comida*
foot	*el pie*
for	*para*
forest	*el bosque*
fork	*el tenedor*
forty	*cuarenta*
four	*cuatro*
fourteen	*catorce*
french fries	*las papas fritas*
Friday	*viernes*
friend	*la amiga* or *el amigo*
from	*de*
fruit	*la fruta*
frying pan	*el sartén*
full	*llena* or *lleno*
fun	*la diversión*

funny	*chistosa* or *chistoso*
furniture	*los muebles*
game	*el juego*
garage	*el garaje*
garden	*el jardín*
gas station	*la gasolinera*
gate	*el portón*
ghost	*el fantasma*
giant	*el gigante*
giraffe	*la jirafa*
girl	*la niña*
glass	*el vaso*
glove	*el guante*
glue	*el pegamento*
God	*Dios*
good	*buena* or *bueno*
good-bye	*adiós*
grandfather	*el abuelo*
grandmother	*la abuela*
grape	*la uva*
grass	*el pasto*
gray	*gris*
green	*verde*
guitar	*la guitarra*
gum	*el chicle*
hair	*el pelo*
hairbrush	*el cepillo*
haircut	*el corte de pelo*
hallway	*el pasillo*
ham	*el jamón*
hamburger	*la hamburguesa*
hammer	*el martillo*
hand	*la mano*
handkerchief	*el pañuelo*
handsome	*guapo*
happy	*feliz*
hard	*dura* or *duro*

has	*tiene*
he	*él*
he is	*él es*
head	*la cabeza*
headache	*el dolor de cabeza*
heart	*el corazón*
helicopter	*el helicóptero*
hello	*hola*
her	*su*
here	*aquí*
highway	*la carretera*
hill	*el cerro*
his	*su*
homework	*la tarea*
honey	*la miel*
horn	*la trompeta*
horse	*el caballo*
hose	*la manguera*
hospital	*el hospital*
hot	*caliente*
hot dog	*el perro caliente*
hotel	*el hotel*
hour	*la hora*
house	*la casa*
hug	*el abrazo*
husband	*esposo*
I	*yo*
I am	*yo estoy* or *yo soy*
ice	*el hielo*
ice cream	*el helado*
important	*importante*
in front	*enfrente*
in	*en*
inside	*adentro*
it is	*es* or *está*
jacket	*la chaqueta*
January	*enero*

jello	*la gelatina*
joke	*el chiste*
juice	*el jugo*
July	*julio*
June	*junio*
key	*la llave*
king	*el rey*
kiss	*el beso*
kitchen	*la cocina*
kite	*la cometa*
kitty	*el gatito*
knife	*el cuchillo*
ladder	*la escalera*
lady (Mrs.)	*Señora (Sra.)*
lake	*el lago*
lamp	*la lámpara*
language	*el lenguaje*
last	*última* or *último*
late	*tarde*
later	*luego*
lazy	*perezosa* or *perezoso*
leaf	*la hoja*
left	*izquierda*
leg	*la pierna*
lemonade	*la limonada*
less	*menos*
lettuce	*la lechuga*
library	*la biblioteca*
lights	*las luces*
lion	*la leona* or *el león*
little	*chica* or *chico*
living room	*la sala*
long	*larga* or *largo*
love	*el amor*
lunch	*el almuerzo*
magazine	*la revista*
magic	*la magia*

mail carrier	*el cartero*
mail	*el correo*
mailbox	*el buzón*
man	*el hombre*
many	*muchas* or *muchos*
map	*el mapa*
March	*marzo*
marker	*el marcador*
math	*las matemáticas*
May	*mayo*
meat	*la carne*
mechanic	*el* or *la mecánico*
medicine	*la medicina*
merry-go-round	*los caballitos*
milk	*la leche*
milk shake	*el batido*
minute	*el minuto*
mirror	*el espejo*
Miss (Ms.)	*Señorita (Srta.)*
Mister (Mr.)	*Señor (Sr.)*
Monday	*lunes*
money	*el dinero*
monster	*el monstruo*
month	*el mes*
moon	*la luna*
mop	*el trapeador*
more	*más*
morning	*la mañana*
mother	*la madre*
motorcycle	*la motocicleta*
mountain	*la montaña*
mouse	*el ratón*
mouth	*la boca*
movies	*el cine*
mud	*el lodo*
music	*la música*
my	*mi*

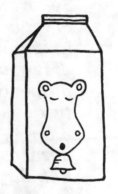

nail	*el clavo*
name	*el nombre*
napkin	*la servilleta*
near	*cerca*
necessary	*necesaria* or *necesario*
neck	*el cuello*
necklace	*el collar*
neighbor	*el vecino*
never	*nunca*
new	*nueva* or *nuevo*
newspaper	*el periódico*
nice	*simpática* or *simpático*
night	*la noche*
nine	*nueve*
nineteen	*diecinueve*
ninety	*noventa*
no	*no*
nobody	*nadie*
none	*ninguna* or *ninguno*
nose	*la nariz*
not	*no*
notebook	*el cuaderno*
nothing	*nada*
November	*noviembre*
now	*ahora*
number	*el número*
nurse	*la enfermera* or *el enfermero*
October	*octubre*
of	*de*
office	*la oficina*
old	*vieja* or *viejo*
on	*en*
one	*uno*
one hundred	*cien*
one thousand	*mil*
onion	*la cebolla*
only	*sólo* or *solamente*

open	*abierta* or *abierto*
or	*o*
orange (color)	*anaranjada* or *anaranjado*
orange (fruit)	*la naranja*
our	*nuestra* or *nuestro*
outside	*afuera*
overcoat	*el abrigo*
page	*la página*
paint	*la pintura*
pajamas	*el pijama*
pants	*los pantalones*
paper	*el papel*
parents	*los padres*
park	*el parque*
party	*la fiesta*
pen	*el lapicero*
pencil	*el lápiz*
pencil sharpener	*el sacapuntas*
people	*la gente*
pepper	*la pimienta*
person	*la persona*
pet	*el animal doméstico*
phone number	*el número de teléfono*
photo	*la foto*
pie	*el pastel*
pig	*el puerco*
pillow	*la almohada*
pilot	*la* or *el piloto*
pink	*rosada* or *rosado*
place	*el lugar*
plane	*el avión*
planet	*el planeta*
plant	*la planta*
plate	*el plato*
playground	*el campo de recreo*
please	*por favor*
pliers	*las pinzas*

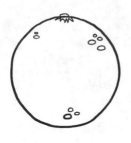

police	*la policía*
police officer	*el policía*
pool	*la piscina*
poor	*pobre*
popcorn	*las palomitas*
possible	*posible*
post office	*la oficina de correo*
pot	*la olla*
potato	*la papa*
present	*el regalo*
pretty	*bonita* or *bonito*
prince	*el príncipe*
princess	*la princesa*
proud	*orgullosa* or *orgulloso*
puppy	*la perrita* or *el perrito*
purple	*morada* or *morado*
purse	*la bolsa*
puzzle	*el rompecabezas*
queen	*la reina*
rabbit	*la coneja* or *el conejo*
radio	*el radio*
rain	*la lluvia*
raincoat	*el impermeable*
rake	*el rastrillo*
reading	*la lectura*
red	*roja* or *rojo*
refrigerator	*el refrigerador*
restaurant	*el restaurante*
restroom	*el servicio*
ribbon	*la cinta*
rice	*el arroz*
rich	*rica* or *rico*
right	*derecha* or *derecho*
ring	*el anillo*
river	*el río*
road	*el camino*
robot	*el robot*

rock	*la roca*
rocket	*el cohete*
room	*el cuarto*
sad	*triste*
salad	*la ensalada*
salesperson	*la vendedora* or *el vendedor*
salt	*la sal*
same	*misma* or *mismo*
sandwich	*el sandwich*
Saturday	*sábado*
saucer	*el platillo*
sausage	*la salchicha*
saw	*el serrucho*
scarf	*la bufanda*
school	*la escuela*
science	*la ciencia*
scissors	*las tijeras*
screwdriver	*el destornillador*
sea	*el mar*
second	*el segundo*
secretary	*la secretaria* or *el secretario*
seesaw	*el subibaja*
September	*septiembre*
seven	*siete*
seventeen	*diecisiete*
seventy	*setenta*
shampoo	*el champú*
she	*ella*
she is	*ella es*
sheep	*la oveja*
sheet	*la sábana*
ship	*el barco*
shirt	*la camisa*
shoes	*los zapatos*
short	*baja* or *bajo*
shorts	*los pantalones cortos*
shoulder	*el hombro*

shovel	*la pala*
shower	*la ducha*
side	*el lado*
sidewalk	*la acera*
sign	*el letrero*
sink	*el lavabo*
sister	*la hermana*
six	*seis*
sixteen	*dieciséis*
sixty	*sesenta*
size	*el tamaño*
skateboard	*la patineta*
skates	*los patines*
skirt	*la falda*
slide	*el resbalador*
slippers	*las pantuflas*
slow	*lenta* or *lento*
smart	*inteligente*
smile	*la sonrisa*
snail	*el caracol*
snake	*la culebra*
snow	*la nieve*
soap	*el jabón*
soccer	*el fútbol*
social studies	*los estudios sociales*
socks	*los calcetines*
soda	*el refresco*
soldier	*el soldado*
some	*algunas* or *algunos*
someone	*alguien*
something	*algo*
sometimes	*a veces*
son	*el hijo*
song	*la canción*
soon	*pronto*
soup	*la sopa*
space	*el espacio*

Spanish	*el español*
special	*especial*
spider	*la araña*
sponge	*la esponja*
spoon	*la cuchara*
sports	*los deportes*
spring	*la primavera*
stairs	*las escaleras*
star	*la estrella*
state	*el estado*
steak	*el bistec*
stereo	*el estéreo*
stomach	*el estómago*
stomachache	*el dolor de estómago*
stone	*la piedra*
store	*la tienda*
story	*el cuento*
stove	*la estufa*
strawberry	*la fresa*
street	*la calle*
strong	*fuerte*
student	*la* or *el estudiante*
stuffed animal	*el animal de peluche*
subway	*el metro*
sugar	*el azúcar*
suit	*el traje*
Sunday	*domingo*
supermarket	*el supermercado*
sweater	*el suéter*
sweet	*dulce*
swing	*el columpio*
table	*la mesa*
tall	*alta* or *alto*
tea	*el té*
teacher	*la maestra* or *el maestro*
team	*el equipo*
teddy bear	*el osito*

teeth	*los dientes*
telephone	*el teléfono*
television	*el televisor*
ten	*diez*
thanks	*gracias*
that	*esa* or *eso*
the	*el, la, los, las*
their	*su*
then	*entonces*
there	*allí*
thermometer	*el termómetro*
these	*estas* or *estos*
they are	*ellos están* or *ellos son*
thin	*delgada* or *delgado*
thing	*la cosa*
third	*tercera* or *tercero*
thirteen	*trece*
thirty	*treinta*
this	*esta* or *este*
those	*esas* or *esos*
throat	*la garganta*
three	*tres*
Thursday	*jueves*
tie	*la corbata*
tiger	*el tigre*
time	*el tiempo*
tired	*cansada* or *cansado*
to	*a*
to the	*al*
today	*hoy*
together	*juntas* or *juntos*
toilet	*el excusado*
tomato	*el tomate*
tomorrow	*mañana*
tool	*la herramienta*
toothache	*el dolor de muela*
toothbrush	*el cepillo de dientes*

toothpaste	*la pasta de dientes*
towel	*la toalla*
town	*el pueblo*
toy	*el juguete*
traffic light	*el semáforo*
train	*el tren*
trash can	*el bote de basura*
tree	*el árbol*
tricks	*los trucos*
truck	*el camión*
t-shirt	*la camiseta*
Tuesday	*martes*
turkey	*el pavo*
turtle	*la tortuga*
twelve	*doce*
twenty	*veinte*
two	*dos*
ugly	*fea* or *feo*
under	*bajo* or *abajo*
underwear	*la ropa interior*
United States	*Estados Unidos*
up	*arriba*
vacation	*las vacaciones*
vacuum cleaner	*la aspiradora*
vegetables	*los vegetales*
very	*muy*
videos	*los vídeos*
vitamin	*la vitamina*
waiter	*el mesero*
wall	*la pared*
wallet	*la cartera*
washer	*la lavadora*
watch	*el reloj*
water	*el agua*
watermelon	*la sandía*
we	*nosotras* or *nosotros*
weak	*débil*

weather	*el tiempo*
Wednesday	*miércoles*
week	*la semana*
white	*blanca* or *blanco*
wife	*la esposa*
window	*la ventana*
winter	*el invierno*
witch	*la bruja*
with	*con*
without	*sin*
wizard	*el mago*
woman	*la mujer*
word	*la palabra*
work	*el trabajo*
worker	*la trabajadora* or *el trabajador*
world	*el mundo*
yard	*el patio*
year	*el año*
yellow	*amarillo*
yes	*sí*
yesterday	*ayer*
you *(formal)*	*usted*
you *(informal)*	*tú*
you are	*tú eres* or *tú estás*
you guys	*ustedes*
young	*joven*
young person	*muchacha* or *muchacho*
your	*tu*
zero	*cero*
zoo	*el zoológico*

EXPRESSIONS

ENGLISH	ESPAÑOL
And you?	¿Y tú?
At night.	De noche.
At__o'clock	A las ___.
Congratulations!	¡Felicitaciones!
Do you have __?	¿Tienes ___?
Do you know?	¿Sabes?
Do you like it?	¿Te gusta?
Do you need help?	¿Necesitas ayuda?
Do you speak Spanish?	¿Hablas español?
Do you understand?	¿Entiendes?
Do you want __?	¿Quieres ___?
Excuse me.	Con permiso.
Good afternoon.	Buenas tardes.
Good luck!	¡Buena suerte!
Good morning.	Buenos días.
Good night.	Buenas noches.
Happy Birthday!	¡Feliz cumpleaños!
Happy Easter!	¡Felices Pascuas!
Hi!	¡Hola!
How are you?	¿Cómo estás?
How many?	¿Cuántos?
How much?	¿Cuánto?
How old are you?	¿Cuántos años tienes?
How pretty!	¡Qué bonito!
How?	¿Cómo?
How's the weather?	¿Qué tiempo hace?
I don't know.	No sé.

I don't remember.	*No recuerdo.*
I don't understand.	*No entiendo.*
I have it.	*Lo tengo.*
I like it.	*Me gusta.*
I live at__.	*Vivo en ___.*
I need the __.	*Necesito ___.*
I put on the __.	*Me pongo ___.*
I speak a little.	*Hablo un poquito.*
I take off the __.	*Me quito ___.*
I want the __.	*Quiero ___.*
I'm hungry.	*Tengo hambre.*
I'm learning Spanish.	*Estoy aprendiendo español.*
I'm sick.	*Estoy enferma* or *Estoy enfermo.*
I'm sorry.	*Lo siento.*
I'm thirsty.	*Tengo sed.*
It's __ o'clock.	*Son las ___.*
It's cold.	*Hace frío.*
It's hot.	*Hace calor.*
It's raining.	*Está lloviendo.*
It's snowing.	*Está nevando.*
It's sunny.	*Hace sol.*
Let's celebrate.	*Celebremos.*
Let's go to the __.	*Vamos a ___.*
Me, too.	*Yo tambien.*
Merry Christmas!	*¡Feliz Navidad!*
My name is __.	*Me llamo ___.*
Not much.	*Sin novedad.*
See you later.	*Hasta luego.*
Speak more slowly.	*Habla más despacio.*
Sure.	*Claro.*
Thanks a lot.	*Muchas gracias.*
There is/are __.	*Hay ___.*
Very well.	*Muy bien.*
Welcome!	*¡Bienvenidos!*
What color is it?	*¿De qué color es?*
What grade are you in?	*¿En qué grado estás?*
What time is it?	*¿Qué hora es?*

Muchas
gracias.

What?	¿Qué?
What's going on?	¿Qué pasa?
What's the date?	¿Cuál es la fecha?
What's the matter?	¿Qué te pasa?
What's your name?	¿Cómo te llamas?
When?	¿Cuándo?
Where?	¿Dónde?
Where do you live?	¿Dónde vives?
Where is it?	¿Dónde está?
Which?	¿Cuál?
Who?	¿Quién?
Why?	¿Por qué?
You're welcome.	De nada.

De nada.

COMMANDS

ENGLISH	ESPAÑOL
Clean.	*Limpia.*
Come.	*Ven.*
Give me.	*Dame.*
Go.	*Anda.*
Look at.	*Mira.*
Point to.	*Señala.*
Take.	*Toma.*
Bring.	*Trae.*
Eat.	*Come.*
Drink.	*Bebe.*
Put.	*Pon.*
Tell me.	*Dime.*
Touch.	*Toca.*
Wash.	*Lava.*

ENGLISH-SPANISH FLASHCARDS

Use scissors to cut along the dotted lines. Keep the cards together with a rubber band, and put them in a safe place, so you can take them out whenever you want to practice. Start right now!

la lámpara

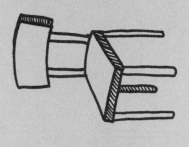

la silla

el tocador

el reloj

el ropero

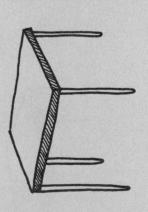

la mesa

chair

lamp

la lampara

clock

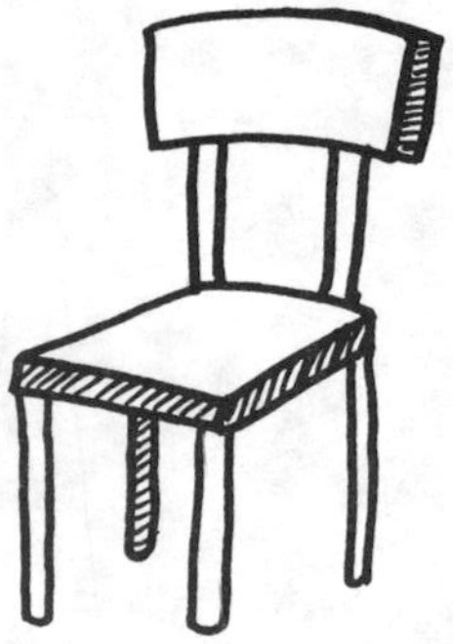

dresser

table

closet

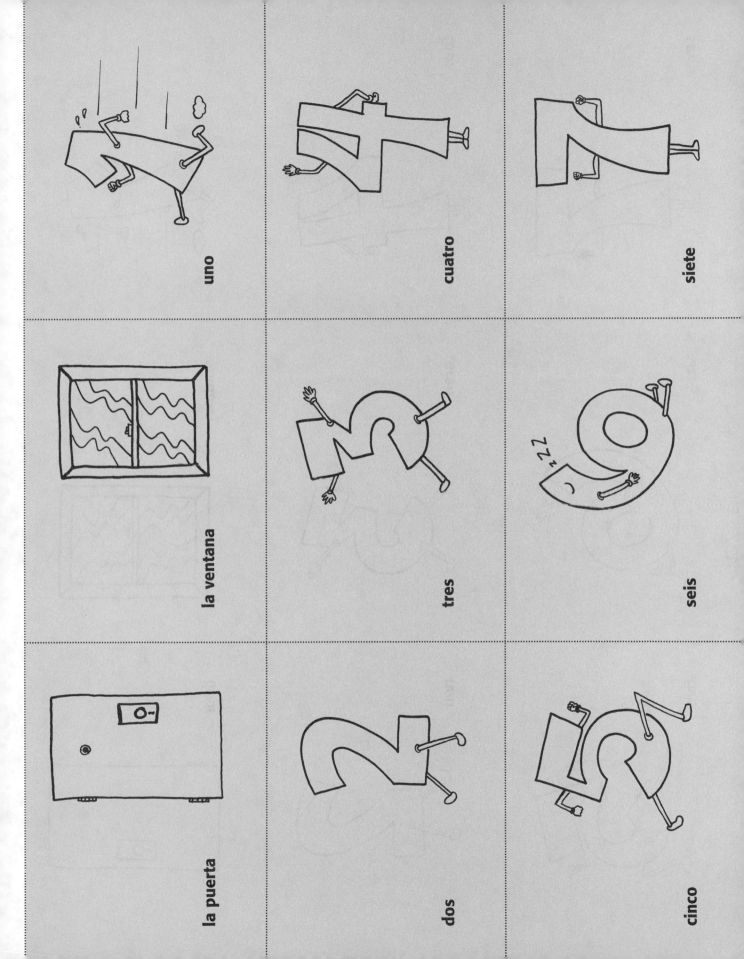

la puerta

la ventana

uno

dos

tres

cuatro

cinco

seis

siete

seven

four

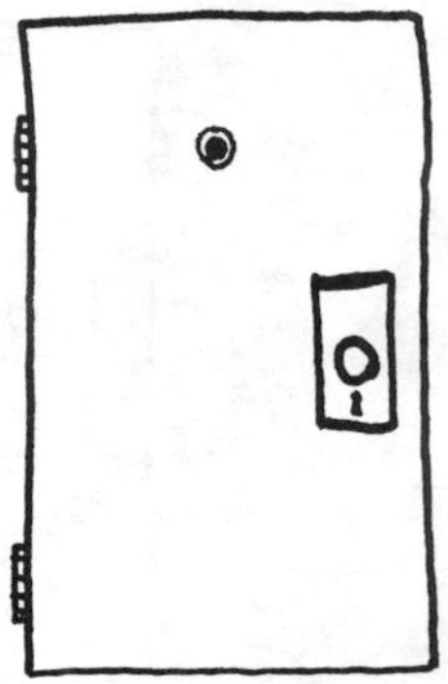

one

six

three

window

five

two

door

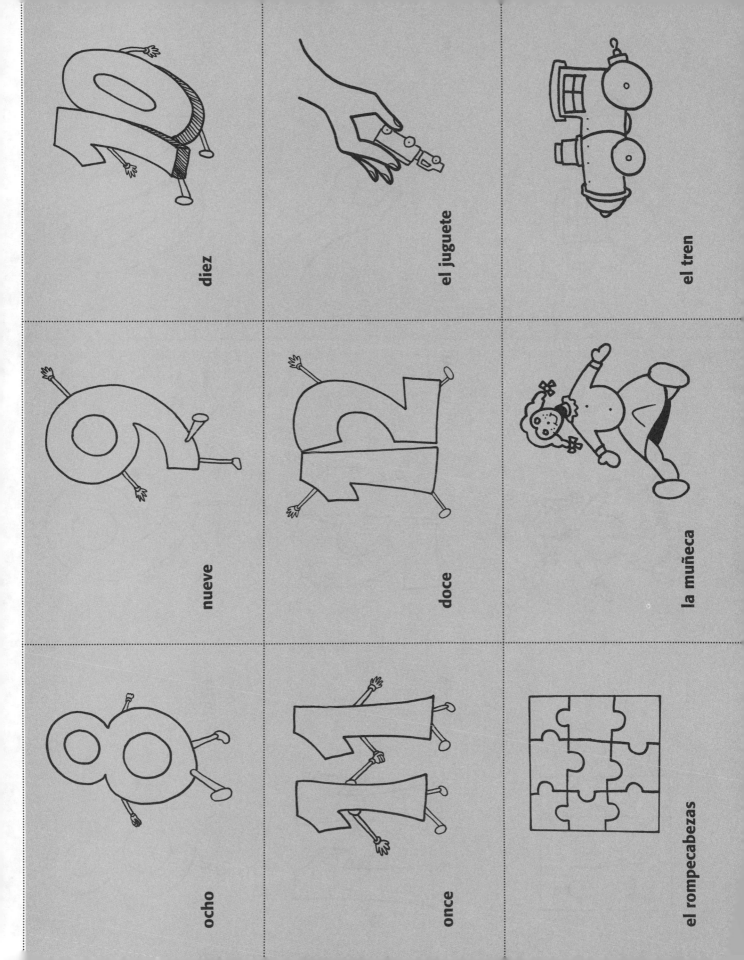

diez

el juguete

el tren

nueve

doce

la muñeca

ocho

once

el rompecabezas

train

toy

ten

doll

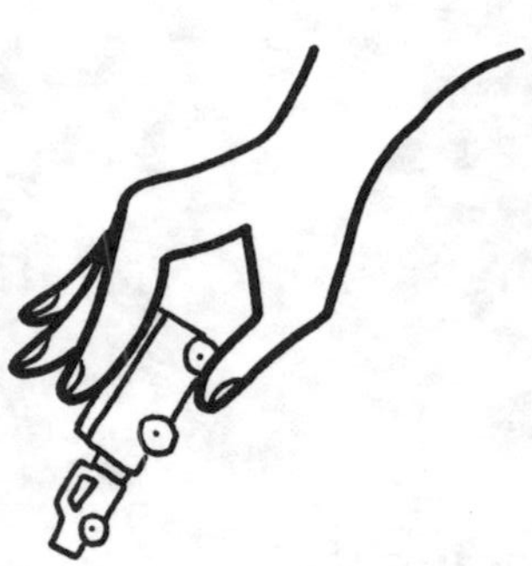

twelve

nine

puzzle

eleven

eight

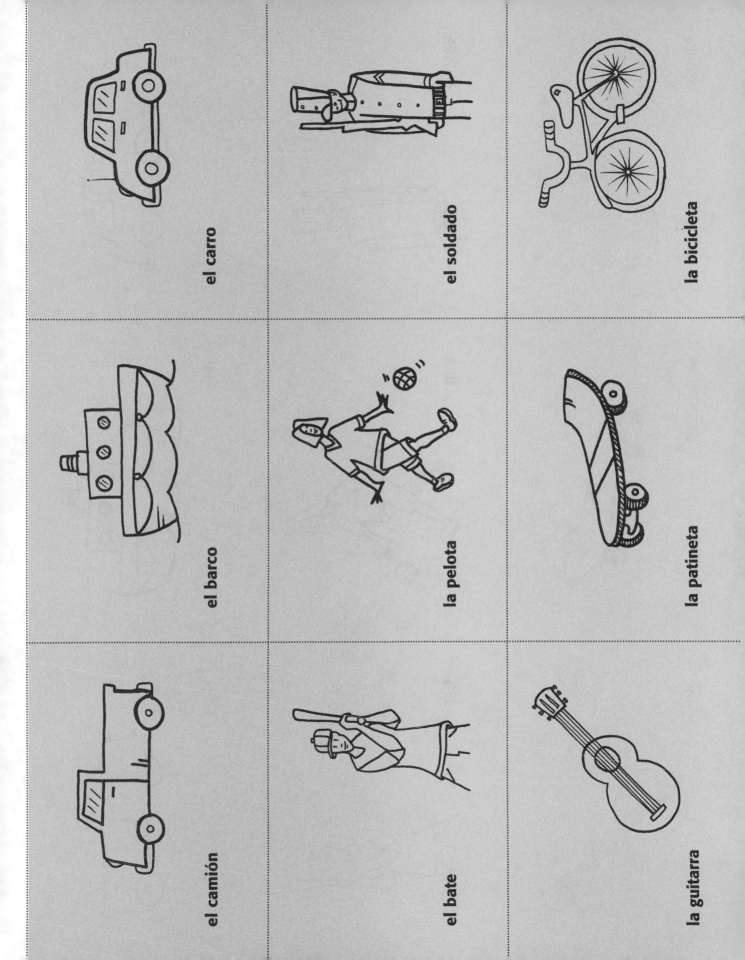

el carro

el soldado

la bicicleta

el barco

la pelota

la patineta

el camión

el bate

la guitarra

bicycle

soldier

car

skateboard

ball

ship

guitar

bat

truck

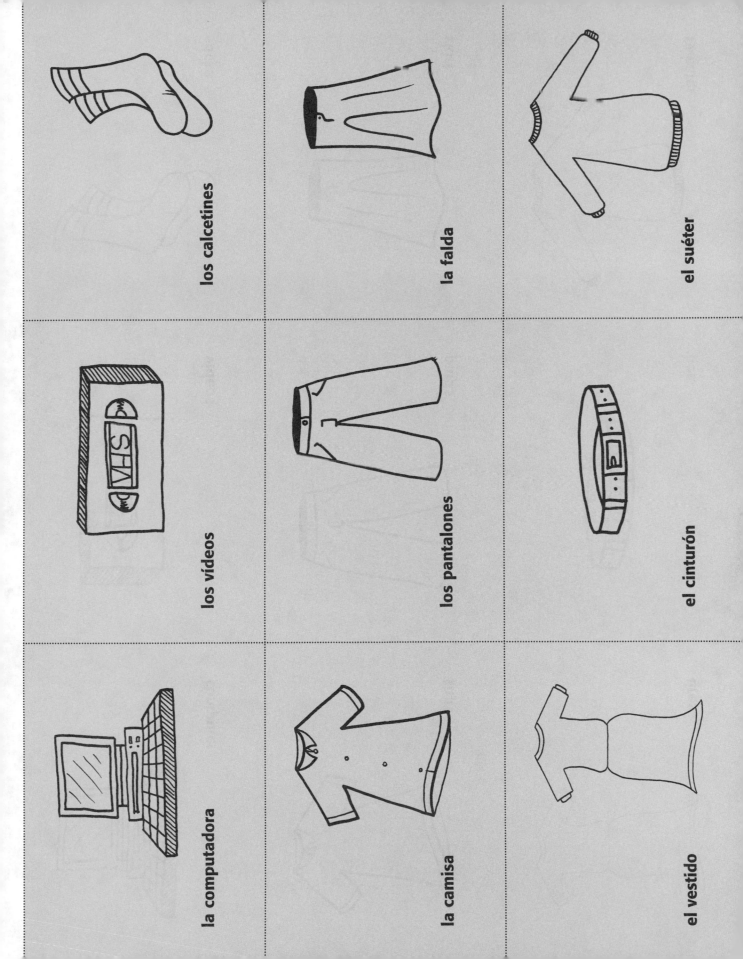

los calcetines

la falda

el suéter

los vídeos

los pantalones

el cinturón

la computadora

la camisa

el vestido

sweater

skirt

socks

belt

pants

videos

dress

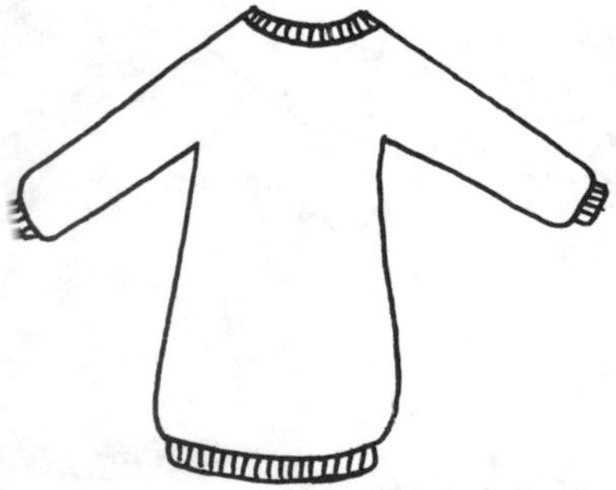

shirt

computer

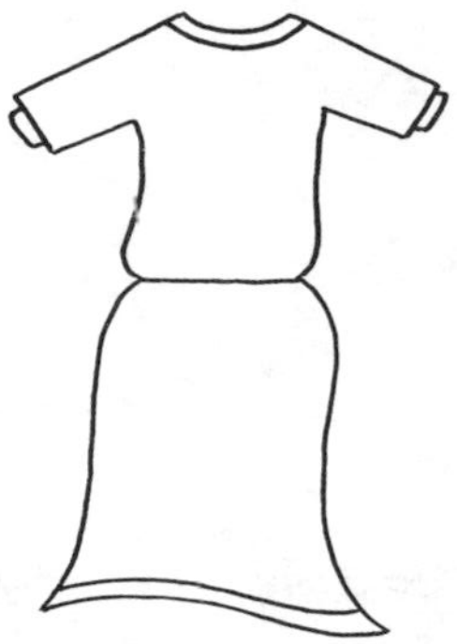

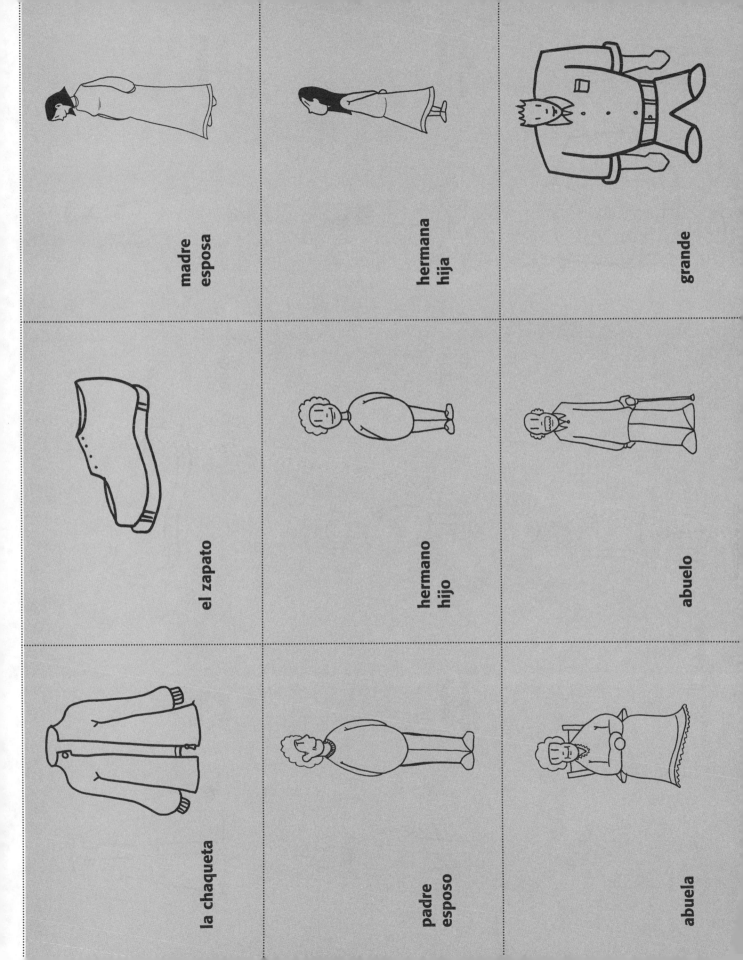

madre
esposa

hermana
hija

grande

el zapato

hermano
hijo

abuelo

la chaqueta

padre
esposo

abuela

big

sister
daughter

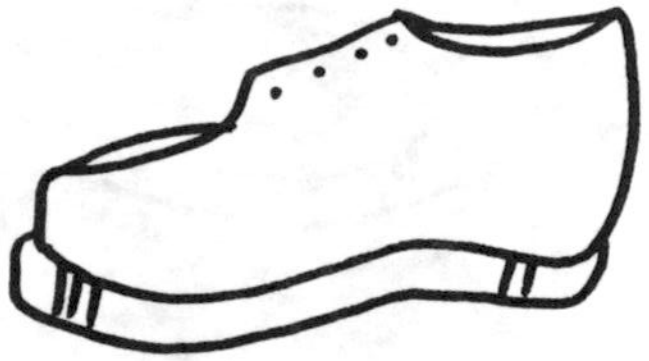

mother
wife

grandfather

brother
son

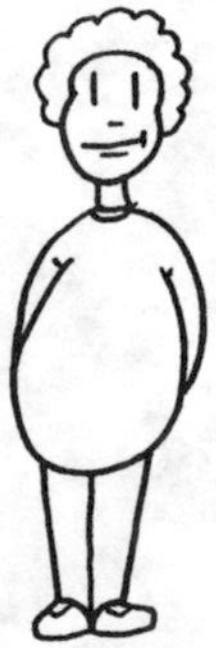

shoe

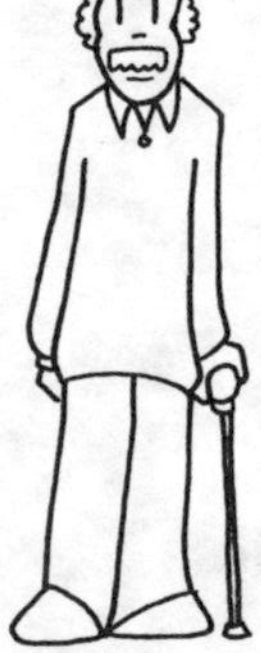

grandmother

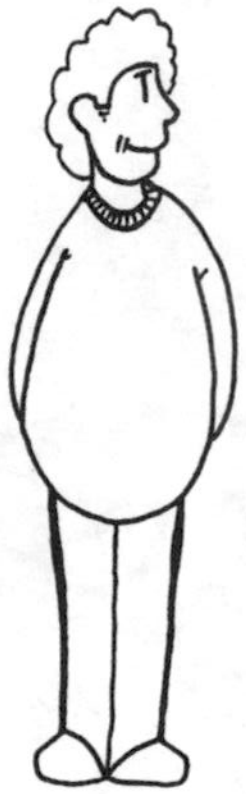

father
husband

jacket

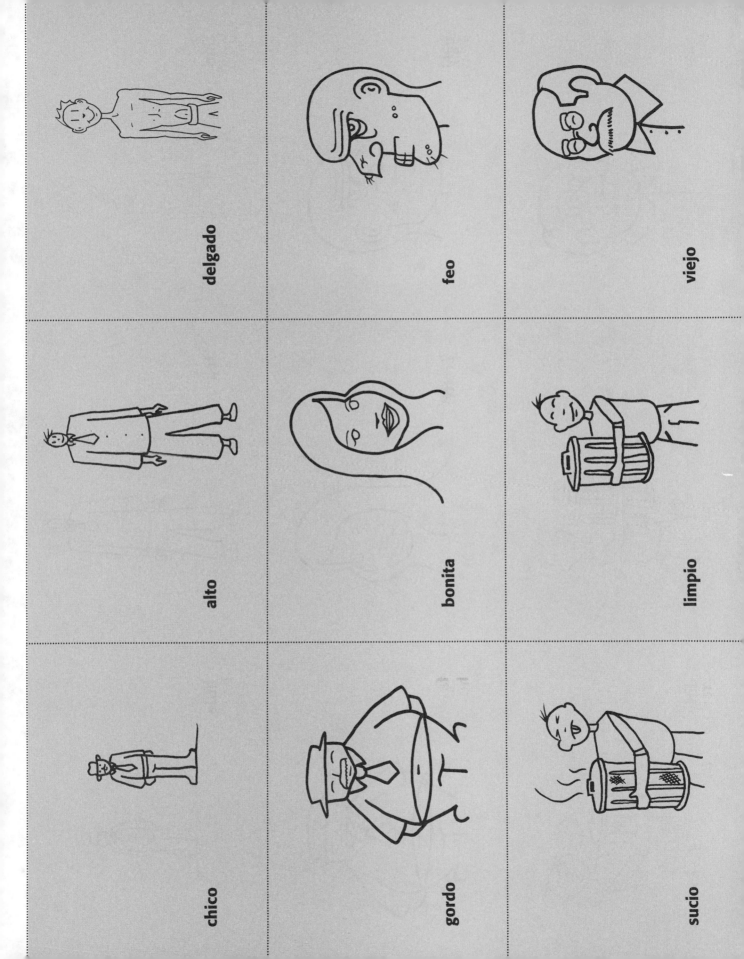

delgado

feo

viejo

alto

bonita

limpio

chico

gordo

sucio

old

ugly

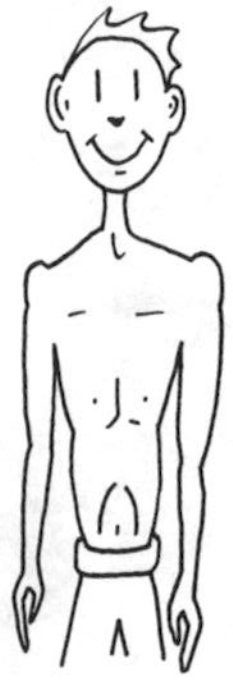

thin

clean

pretty

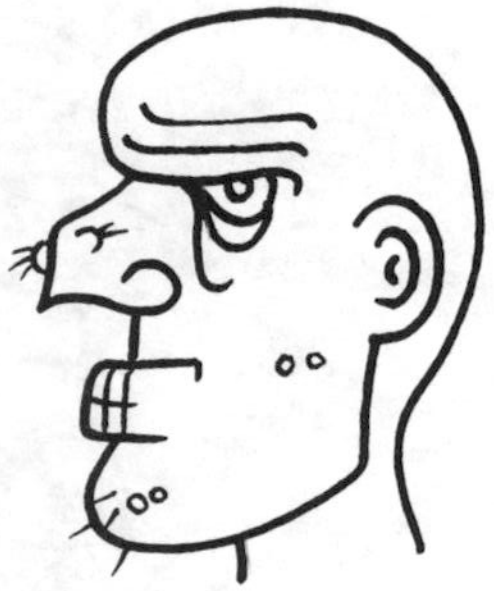

tall

dirty

fat

little

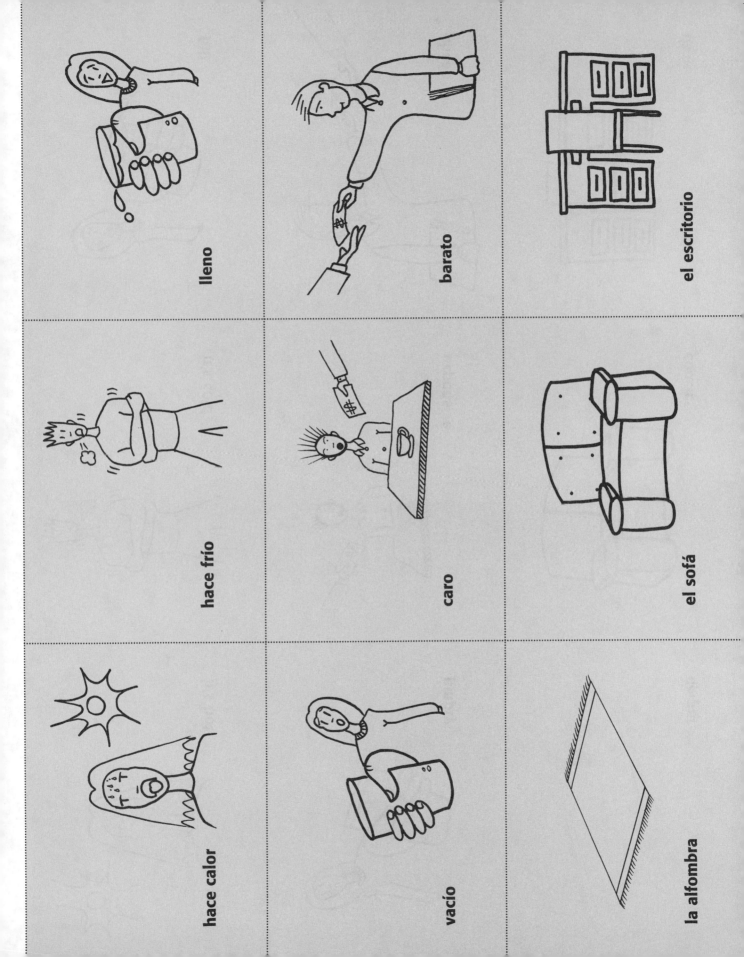

lleno

barato

el escritorio

hace frío

caro

el sofá

hace calor

vacío

la alfombra

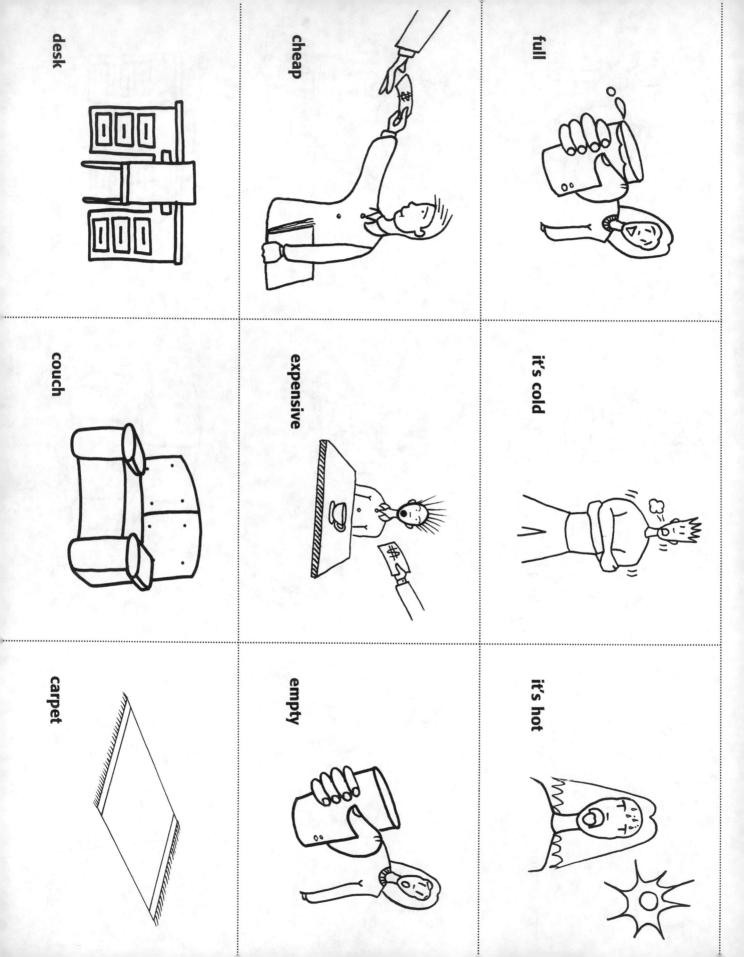

full

cheap

desk

it's cold

expensive

couch

it's hot

empty

carpet

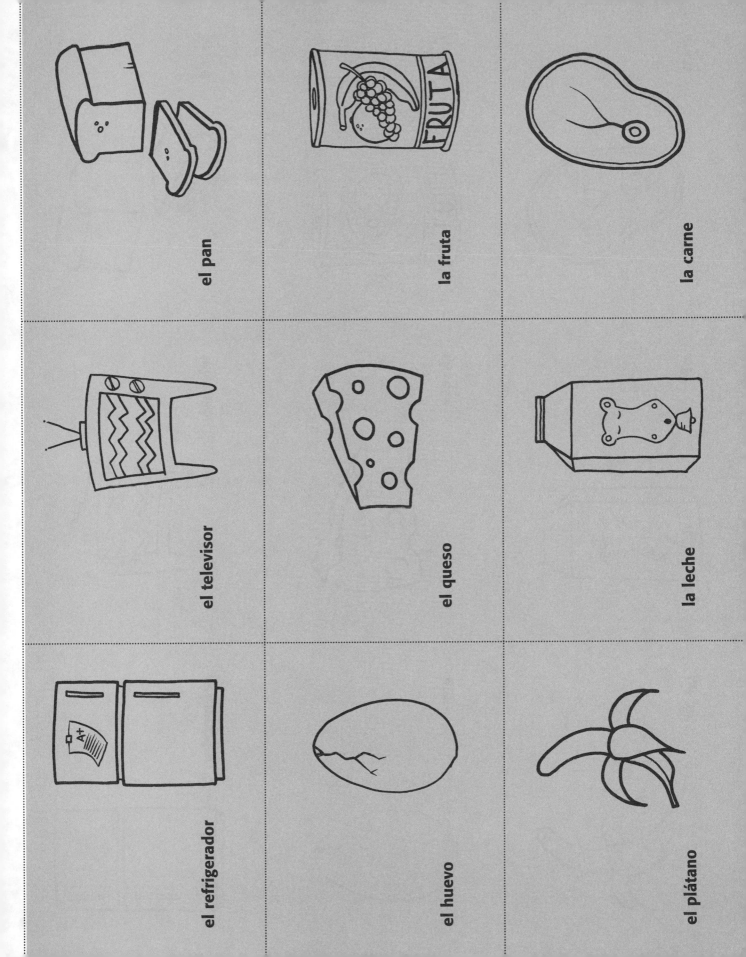

el pan

la fruta

la carne

el televisor

el queso

la leche

el refrigerador

el huevo

el plátano

meat

fruit

FRUTA

bread

milk

cheese

television

banana

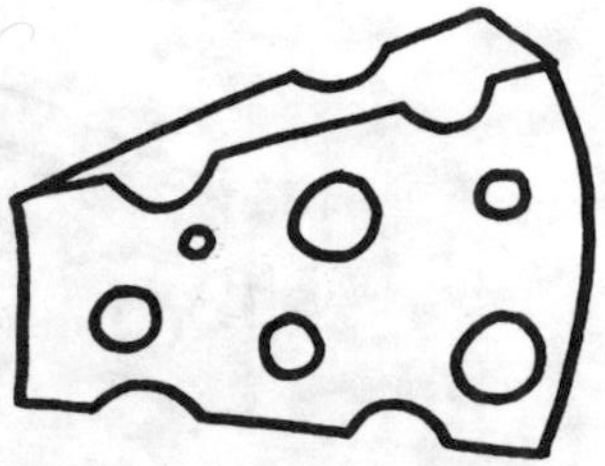

egg

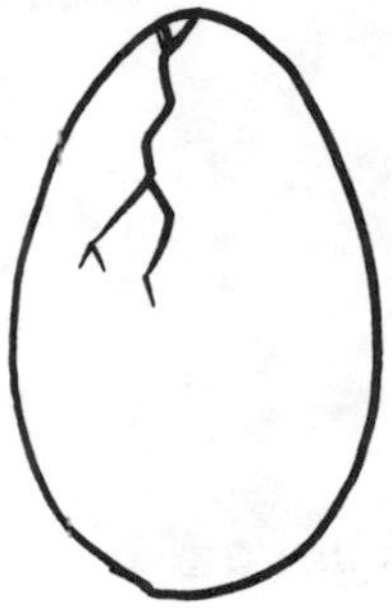

refrigerator

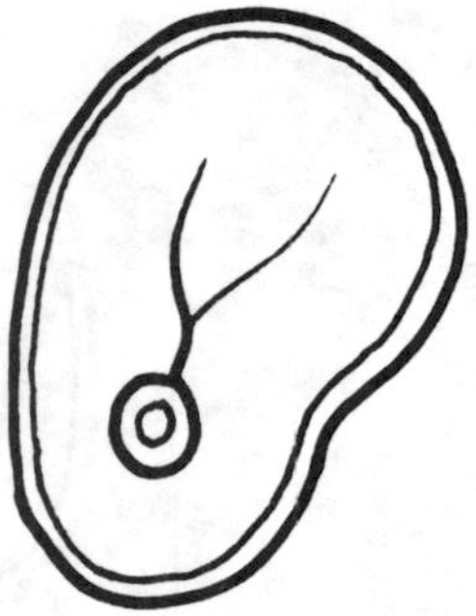

A+

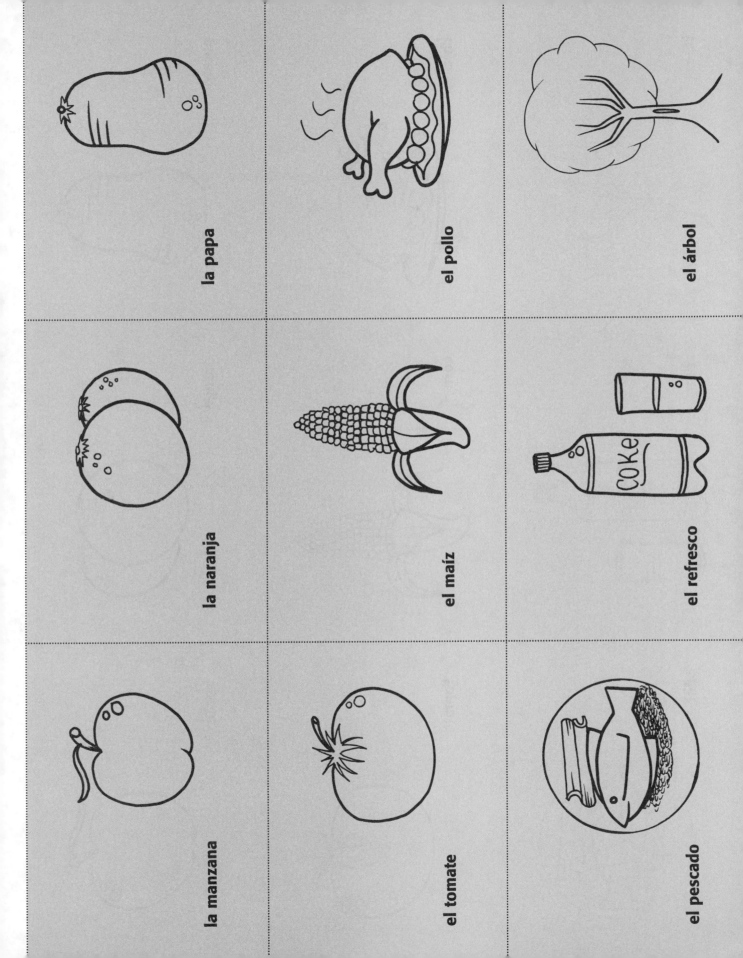

la papa

el pollo

el árbol

la naranja

el maíz

el refresco

la manzana

el tomate

el pescado

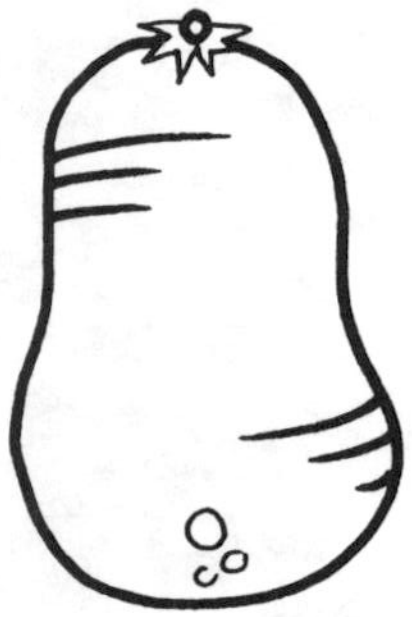

tree

chicken

potato

soda

corn

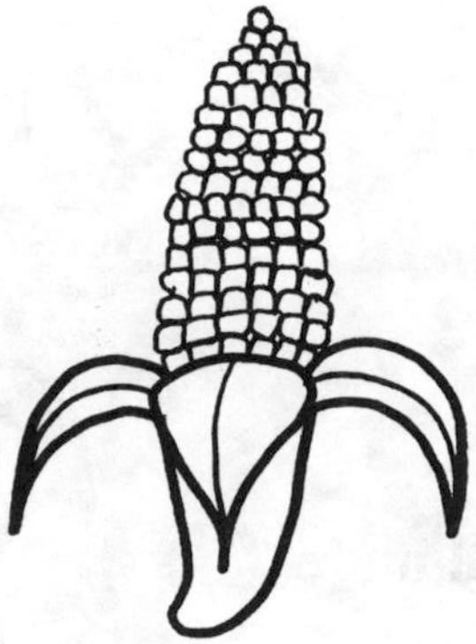

orange

fish

tomato

apple

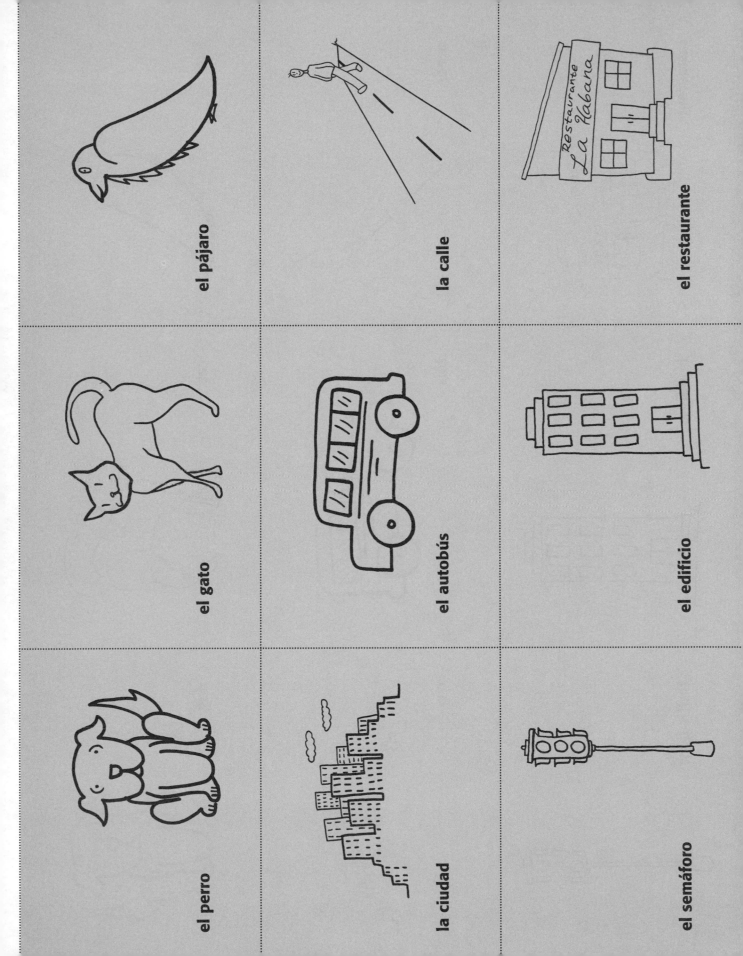

el pájaro

la calle

el restaurante

el gato

el autobús

el edificio

el perro

la ciudad

el semáforo

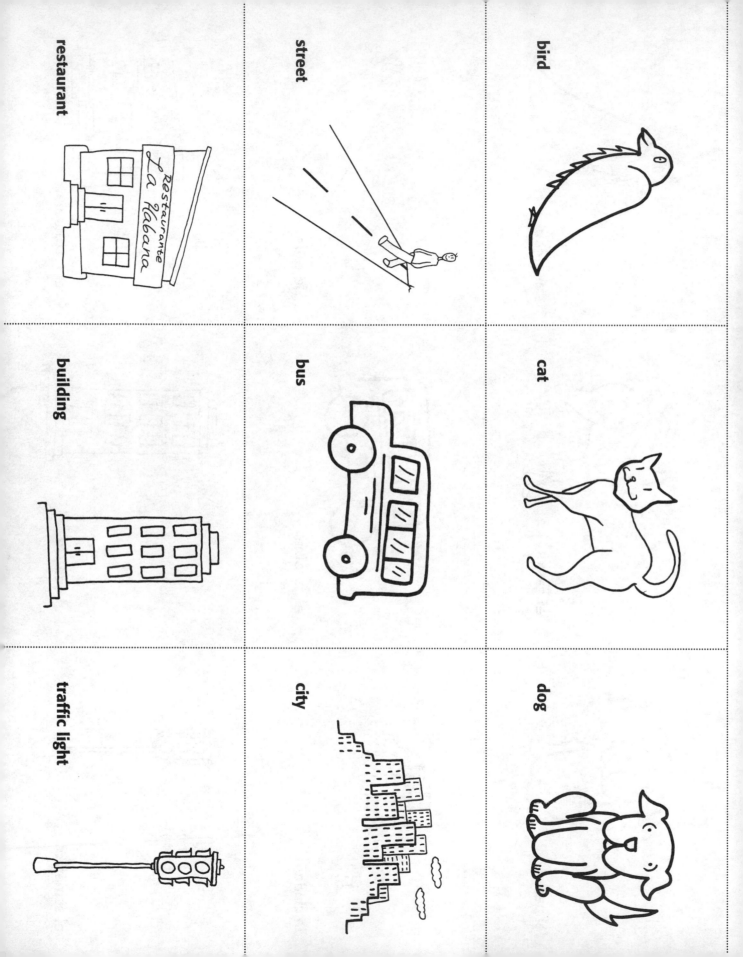

bird

street

restaurant

Restaurante La Habana

cat

bus

building

dog

city

traffic light

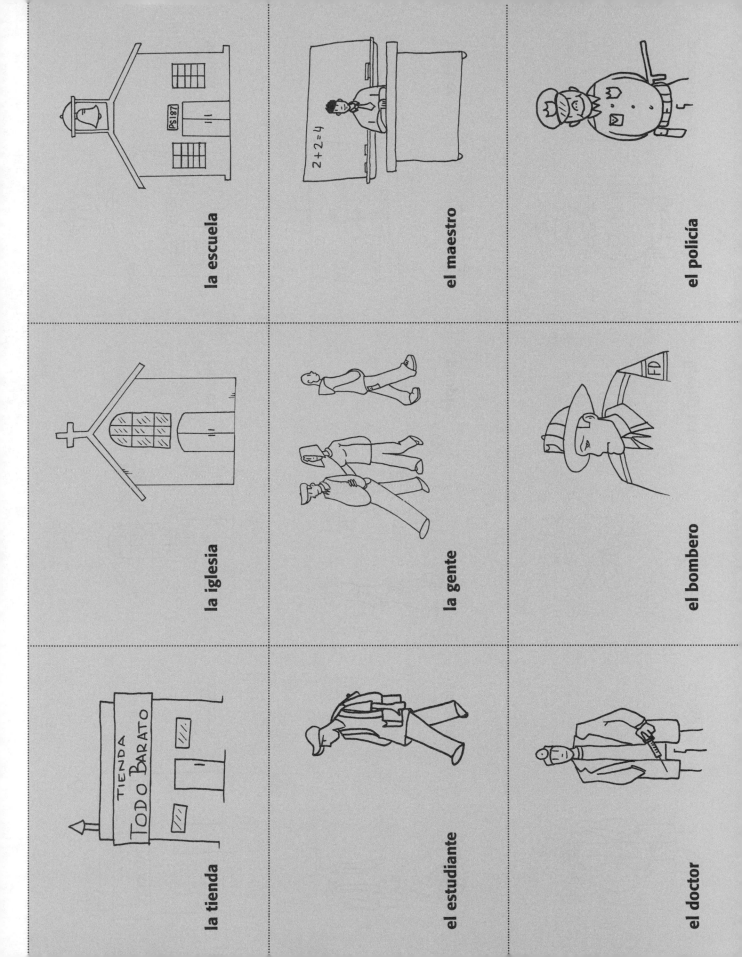

la escuela

el maestro

el policía

la iglesia

la gente

el bombero

la tienda

TIENDA TODO BARATO

el estudiante

el doctor

school

teacher

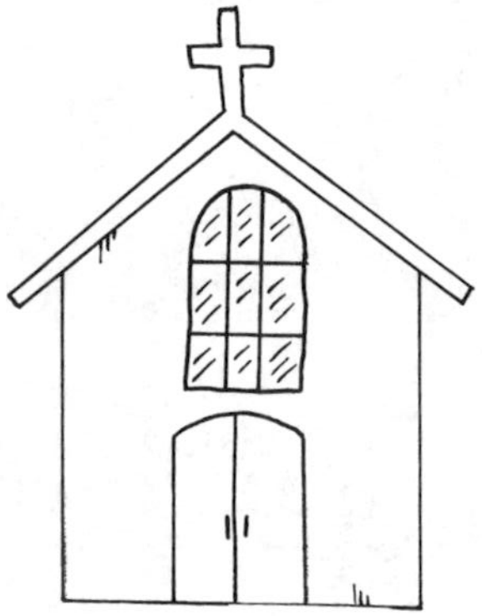

police officer

church

people

firefighter

store

student

doctor

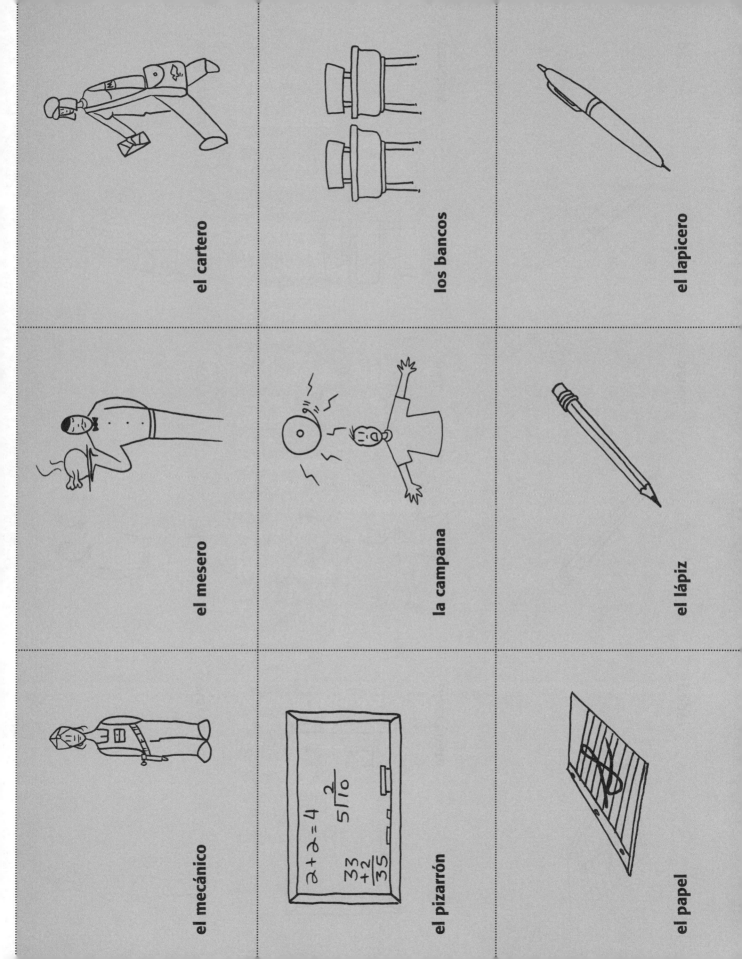

el cartero

los bancos

el lapicero

el mesero

la campana

el lápiz

el mecánico

el pizarrón

el papel

mail carrier

benches

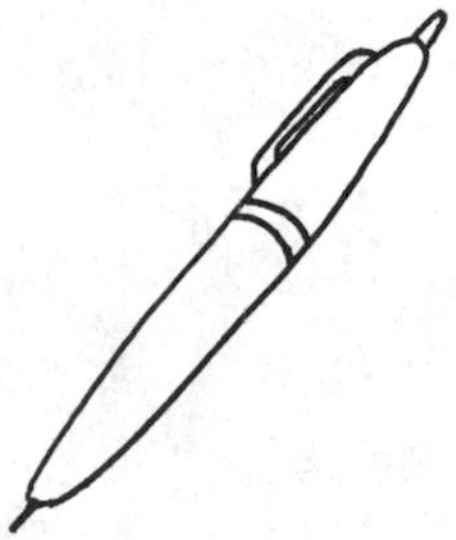

pen

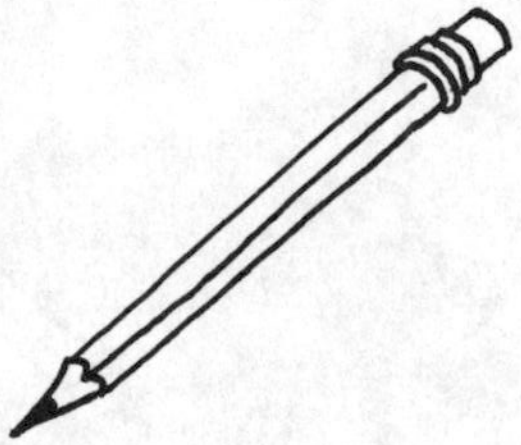

waiter

bell

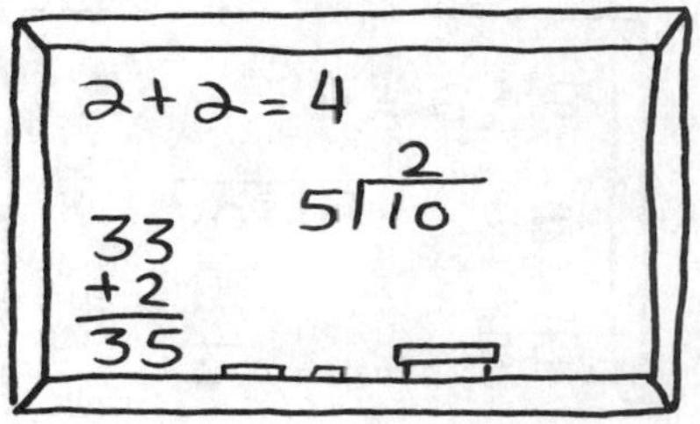

pencil

mechanic

blackboard

$2 + 2 = 4$

$$\frac{33}{+\ 2}$$
35

2
$5\overline{)10}$

paper

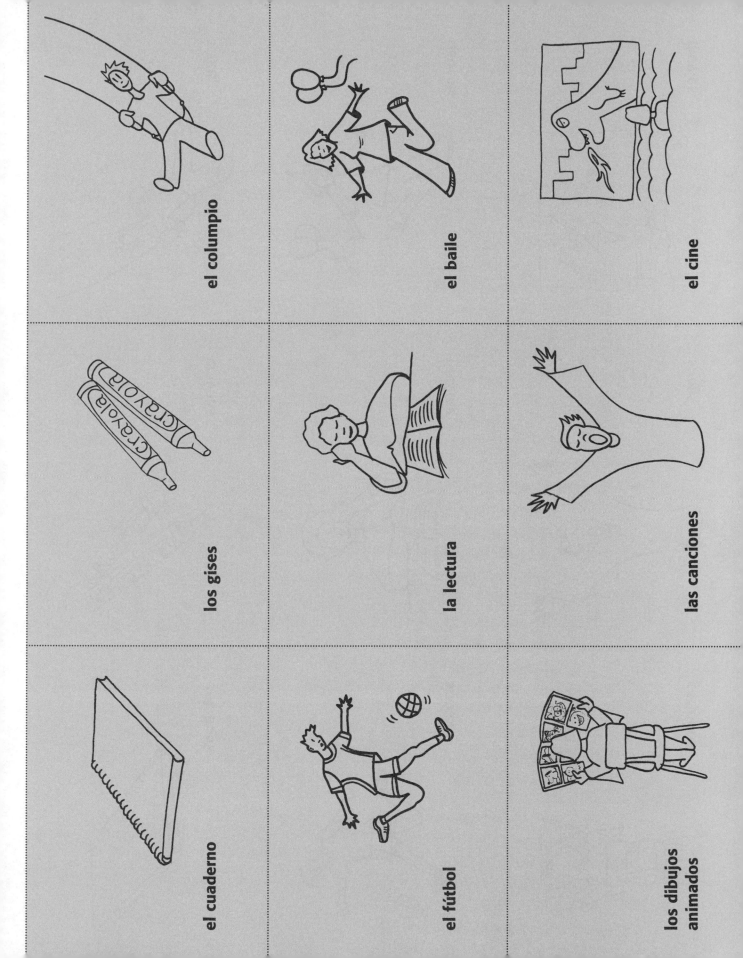

el columpio

el baile

el cine

los gises

la lectura

las canciones

el cuaderno

el fútbol

los dibujos
animados

movies

dancing

swing

songs

reading

crayons

cartoons

soccer

notebook

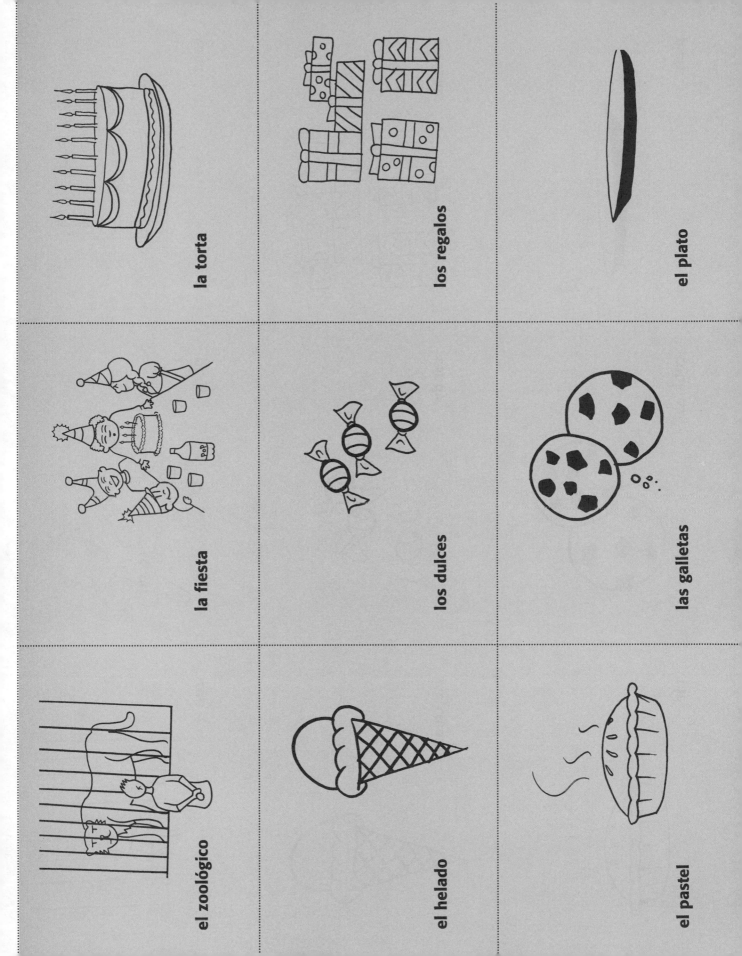

la torta

los regalos

el plato

la fiesta

los dulces

las galletas

el zoológico

el helado

el pastel

plate

presents

cake

cookies

candy

party

pie

ice cream

zoo

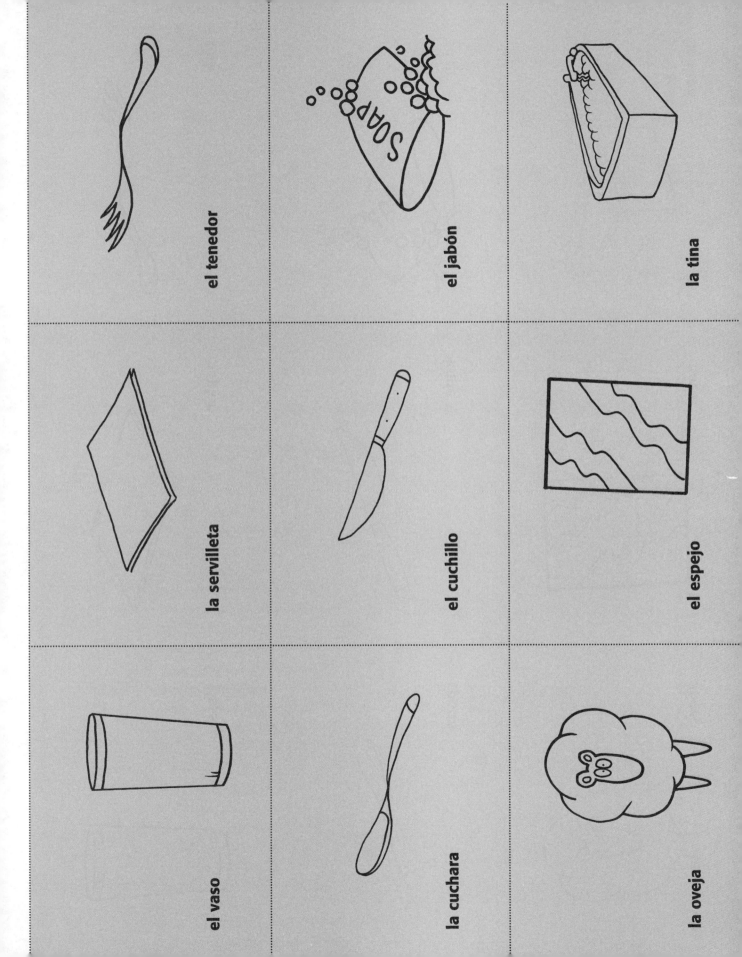

el tenedor

el jabón

la tina

la servilleta

el cuchillo

el espejo

el vaso

la cuchara

la oveja

bathtub

soap

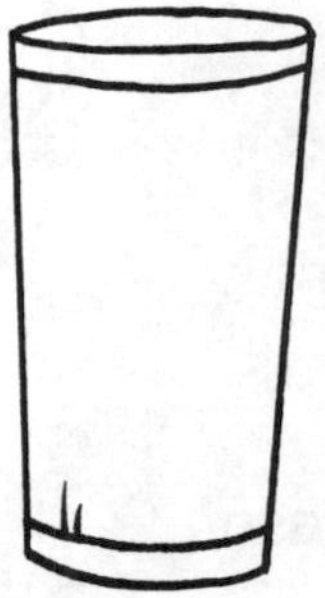

SOAP

fork

mirror

knife

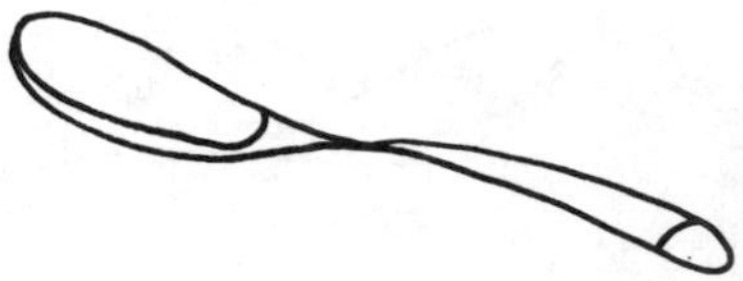

napkin

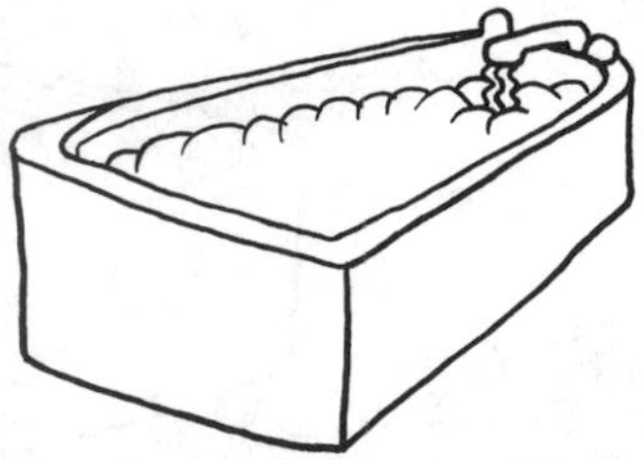

sheep

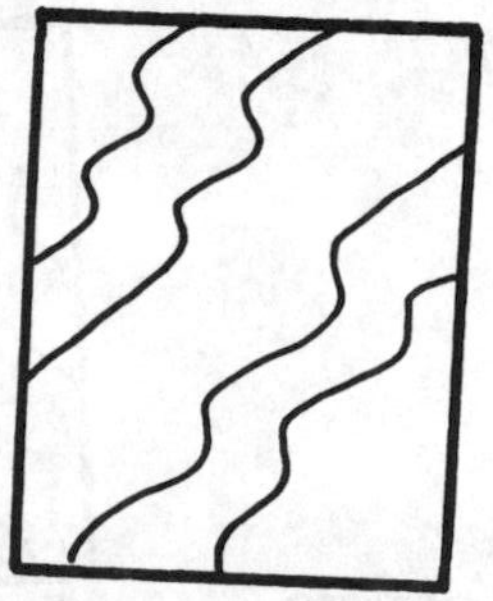

spoon

glass

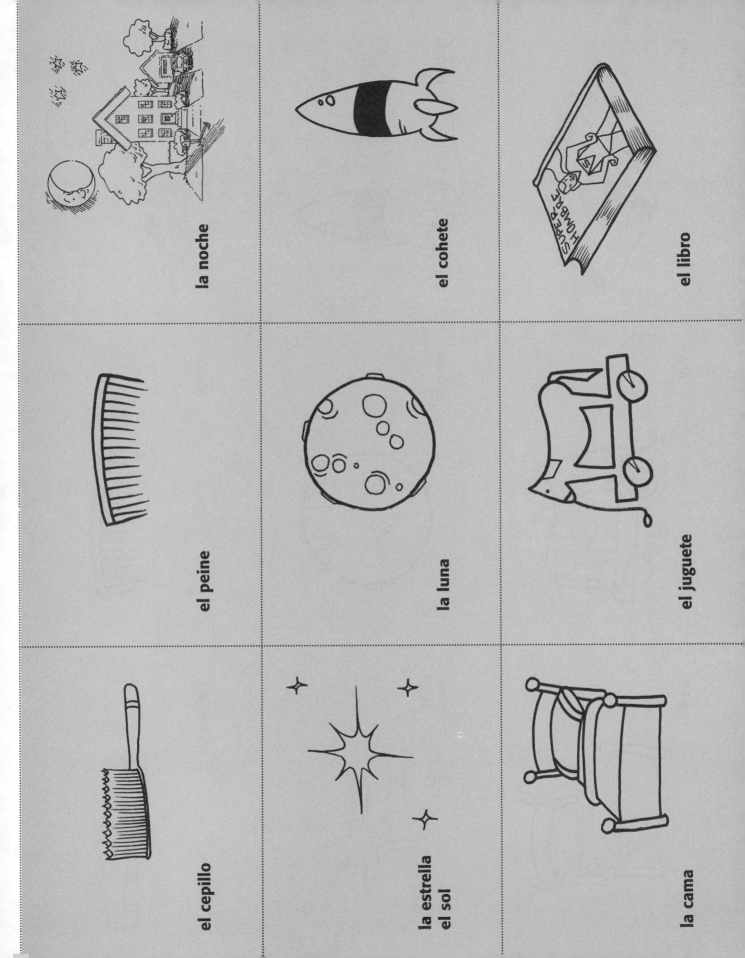

la noche

el cohete

el libro

el peine

la luna

el juguete

el cepillo

la estrella
el sol

la cama

book

rocket

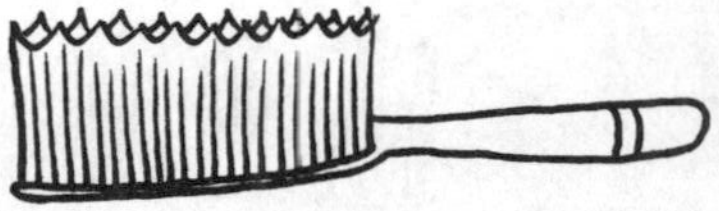

night

toy

moon

comb

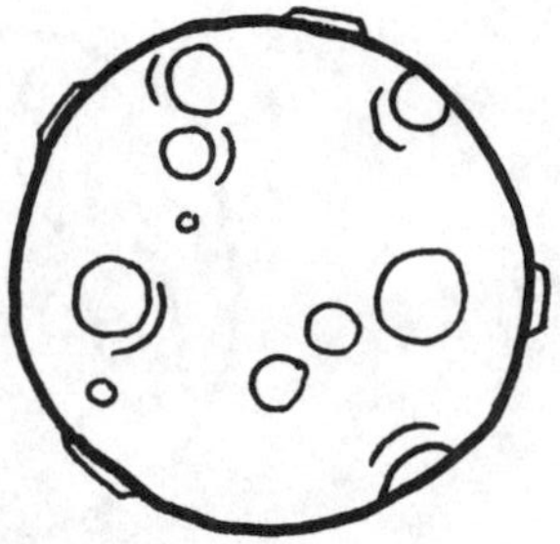

bed

star
sun

hairbrush

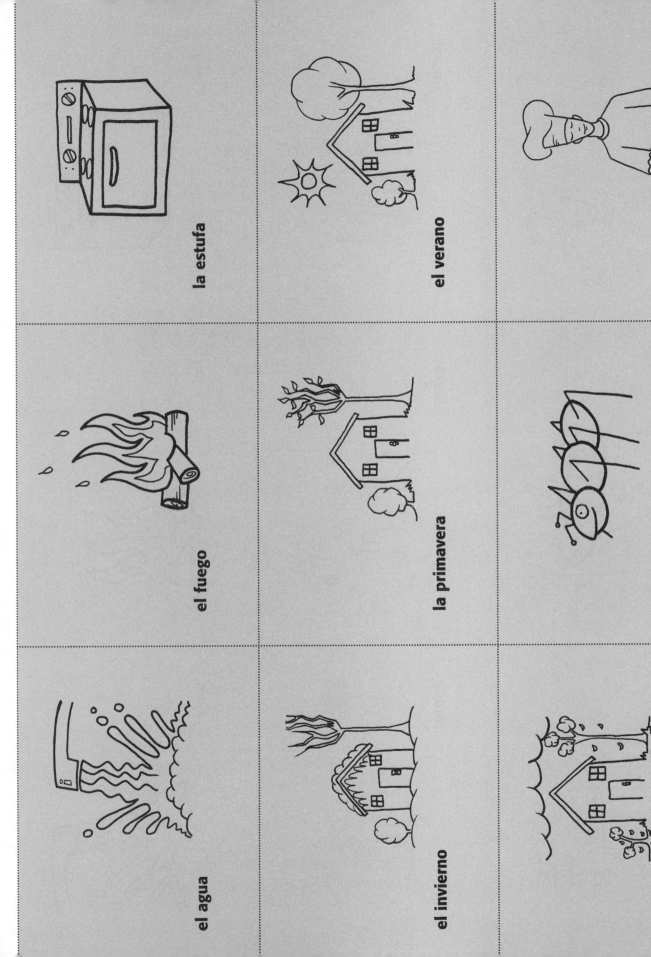

la estufa

el verano

el cocinero

el fuego

la primavera

la hormiga

el agua

el invierno

el otoño

cook

summer

stove

ant

spring

fire

fall

winter

water